WON

BURGUNDY

Text **Jean-François Bazin** Photographs **Hervé Champollion**

Translation **id2m**

Éditions **OUEST-FRANCE**

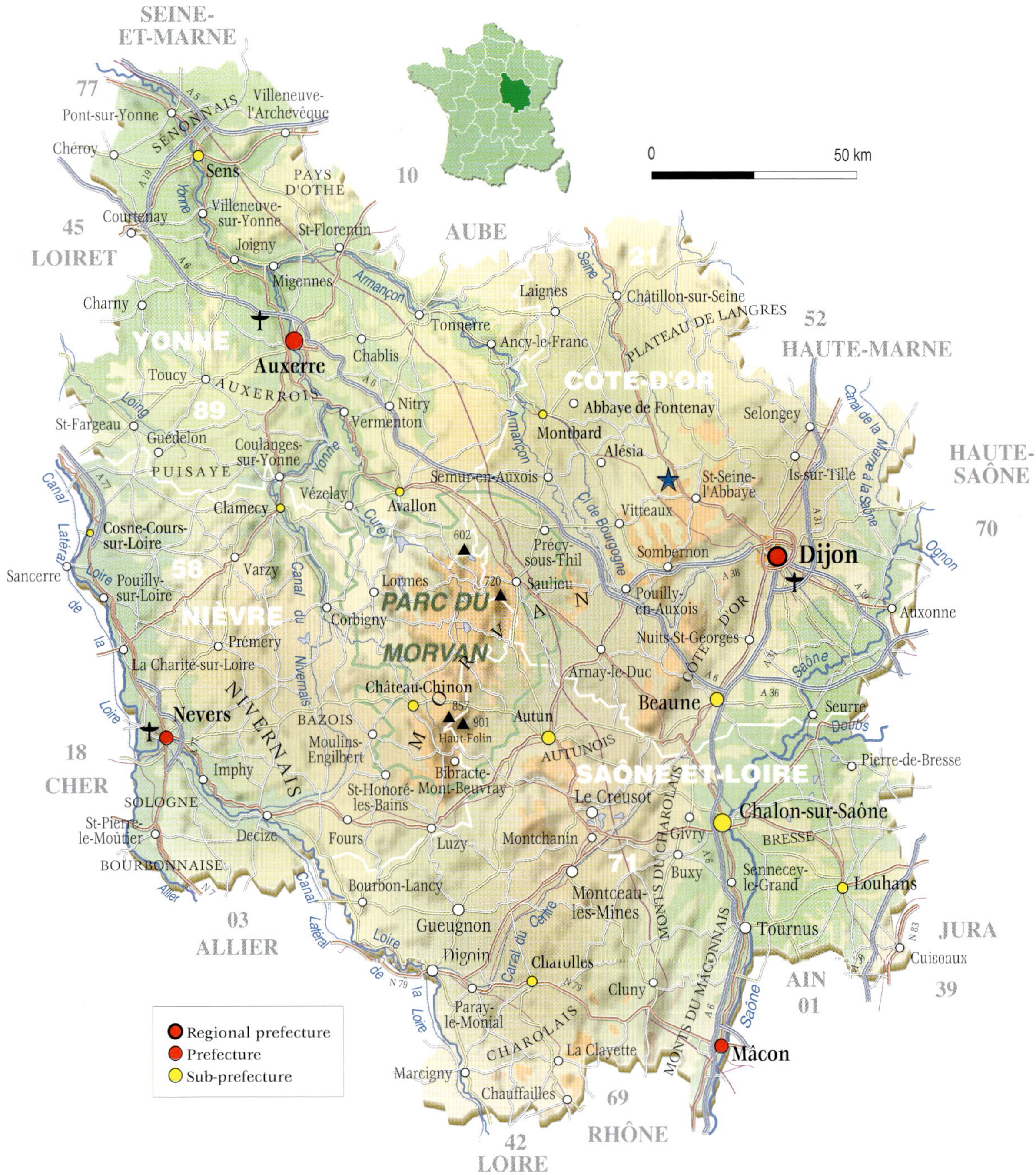
SEINE-
ET-MARNE
77
10
AUBE
45
LOIRET
52
HAUTE-MARNE
HAUTE-
SAÔNE
70
18
CHER
03
ALLIER
42
LOIRE
69
RHÔNE
AIN
01
JURA
39
0
50 km
YONNE
89
NIÈVRE
58
CÔTE-D'OR
21
SAÔNE-ET-LOIRE
71
PARC DU
MORVAN
MORVAN
Pont-sur-Yonne
Villeneuve-
l'Archevêque
SENONNAIS
Chéroy
Sens
PAYS
D'OTHE
Courtenay
Villeneuve-
sur-Yonne
Joigny
St-Florentin
Migennes
Armançon
Charny
Auxerre
Tonnerre
Chablis
Laignes
Châtillon-sur-Seine
PLATEAU DE LANGRES
Ancy-le-Franc
Toucy
AUXERROIS
St-Fargeau
Guédelon
Loing
Nitry
Vermenton
Montbard
Abbaye de Fontenay
Selongey
Canal de la Marne à la Saône
Coulanges-
sur-Yonne
PUISAYE
Alésia
Is-sur-Tille
Semur-en-Auxois
St-Seine-
l'Abbaye
Vézelay
Avallon
Clamecy
Cosne-Cours-
sur-Loire
Vitteaux
Canal latéral de la Loire
Cure
602
Précy-
sous-Thil
Sombernon
Dijon
Ognon
Sancerre
Varzy
Pouilly-
sur-Loire
Lormes
720
Saulieu
Pouilly-
en-Auxois
Auxonne
Corbigny
Nuits-St-Georges
CÔTE D'OR
Prémery
La Charité-sur-Loire
Arnay-le-Duc
Canal du Nivernais
NIVERNAIS
Château-Chinon
857
901
Haut-Folin
Autun
Beaune
Saône
Seurre
Doubs
Nevers
BAZOIS
Moulins-
Engilbert
AUTUNOIS
Pierre-de-Bresse
Imphy
Bibracte-
Mont-Beuvray
St-Honoré-
les-Bains
Le Creusot
Chalon-sur-Saône
SOLOGNE
St-Pierre-
le-Moûtier
Decize
Fours
Luzy
Montchanin
Givry
BRESSE
BOURBONNAISE
Buxy
MONTS DU CHAROLAIS
Sennecey-
le-Grand
Louhans
Bourbon-Lancy
Montceau-
les-Mines
Gueugnon
Canal du Centre
Tournus
Digoin
Charolles
Cluny
MONTS DU MÂCONNAIS
Cuiseaux
Paray-
le-Monial
CHAROLAIS
La Clayette
Mâcon
Marcigny
Chauffailles
Regional prefecture
Prefecture
Sub-prefecture

A region with no natural borders

Burgundy is set at a crossroads between the north and south of France. "The Burgundian is a man who contains a thousand others", said late French writer and poet Jacques Lacarrière.

Although merged with Franche-Comté in 2015 bringing the additional départements of Doubs, Jura, Haute-Saône and Territoire-de-Belfort, Burgundy has retained its identity, heart and soul. Its capital is still Dijon of course. Formerly a duchy, a province and finally a region, it has successfully withstood the upheavals of history. Its *départements* – Côte-d'Or, Nièvre, Saône-et-Loire and Yonne – encircle the Morvan mountain range.

The region covers 12,000 square miles and is one of the largest in France, and even Europe. It is larger than the entire country of Belgium. It is also one of the most sparsely populated with just 1,630,000 inhabitants. There is no natural border apart from the river Saône, which used to separate the kingdom from the empire.

Even the name of the region comes from afar.

Here humans and nature coexist peacefully. The history of Burgundy is inextricably linked to its geography. Burgundy has always been a meeting place, a settling place, and has always drawn people from all over. In fact, the motorways and high-speed train lines often follow Roman and Celtic roadways. Burgundy is proof positive that climate can tell a lot about a region. Far from the harshness of the mountains and adventures of the sea, and safe from earthquakes and volcanoes, Burgundy exemplifies balance and serenity.

Its geology comprises marlstone, limestone, sandstone and granite. Its rivers flow into the Atlantic, the English Channel and the Mediterranean. Its roofs are made of lava, flat tiles, curved tiles and slate. The landscape is ever-changing, as if to continu- ally delight the senses. In contrast, the character of the people of Burgundy is steadfast. The region's reputation owes much to the pleasures of fine food and wine, which are its best selling-point. Burgundians are often seen to sing with raised glasses, sometimes out of duty, sometimes out of pleasure. In fact, they are very secretive but will open up after a little coaxing.

Burgundians epitomise the virtues of hospitality and have a great legacy. The Solutreans and Chasséens were two of the most advanced prehistoric civilisations. The body of the Lady of

Left page
The rock of Vergisson, reminiscent of the rock of Solutré in the Mâconnais area. The *Peute*, a mythical bird, is said to have nested here.

Opposite
Romanesque décor on the church of Saint-Julien-de-Jonzy in the Brionnais area (angels with outspread wings on the portal).

Vix, buried twenty-five centuries ago, was discovered in the Châtillonais area alongside the finest and largest bronze vase of Greek antiquity. This testifies to the intensity of trading between the British isles and the Mediterranean. Cluny and Cîteaux, founded at the very start of the second millennium, were followed by thousands of abbeys throughout Christendom, and the spiritual and artistic heritage of the Romanesque world is still alive in Burgundy today. Founded at the turning point between the Middle Ages and the Renaissance, the Order of the Golden Fleece had an influence throughout Europe. The "great dukes of the West" reunited the different regions, cultures and languages, from Charolais to the North Sea and right into the heart of the continent. European architecture in the 14th and 15th centuries was thus predominantly Burgundian.

The Burgundians

The Burgundians settled here at the end of the 5th century. Originally from the Danish island of Bornholm, they roamed from Hungary to the banks of the Rhine for several centuries. The Burgundian ring illustrates the Germanic Nibelungen saga. Driven out by the Huns, they settled in Savoy and spread out throughout the nearby Saône and Rhone river valleys. This ephemeral Burgundy stretched from Langres to Provence. The kingdom, overthrown in 534, was not barbaric but rather had a civilising influence. Burgundy owes its name to this Scandinavian people. ■

Famous names

Burgundy came under definitive French control on the death of Charles the Bold in 1477. The region boasts many famous natives, including Saint Jane Frances of Chantal, the composer Rameau, the Marquise de Sévigné, the bishop and orator Bossuet, the naturalist Buffon, the military architect Vauban, the revolutionary Saint-Just, the mathematician Monge, the statesman Carnot, the painter Greuze, the poet Lamartine, the encyclopaedist Larousse, the engineer Eiffel, the writers Colette and Romain Rolland, the painter Vuillard, Niépce, who invented photography, Marey, one of the founding fathers of cinema, and the Schneiders, industrialists who turned the Le Creusot foundry into a world-renowned steelmaker, to name but a few. The traces of these famous people can be found throughout Burgundy. Bossuet in Seurre, Buffon in Montbard, Vauban in Bazoches and Saint-Léger-Vauban, Niépce in Chalon-sur-Saône and Saint-Loup-de-Varennes, Marey in Beaune and Colette in Puisaye. ■

Burgundy, a region of multiple landscapes

Left page
The "yellow castle" in Aloxe-Corton. The 19th century was marked by glazed tiled roofs.

Below
View from the Signal d'Uchon in Saône-et-Loire with the Carnaval rocks and never-ending plain.

Burgundy offers ever-changing landscapes and is a mosaic of natural areas, each with its own character and soul. Many writers, poets and artists have been inspired by the diversity of Burgundy's natural resources and scenery. Between the Morvan range and Langres plateau, Burgundy is the meeting point between the Seine and the Saône, and the Vosges and the Loire.

Yonne

The Sénonais, the area around Sens and Joigny, owes its name to a Gallic tribe, the Senones, who took Rome in 390 B.C. The Yonne valley is a mirror image of the Ile-de-France and Champagne regions. On one side lie the vast cereal plantations of the Burgundian Gâtinais, while on the other, near Champagne, stands the Pays d'Othe, a plateau pocked with secretive, wooded, cider-producing valleys. Brick also becomes an increas increasingly common feature in houses as you approach Paris.

Up the Yonne river, you come to Auxerrois, where the river becomes navigable. There are white stone hills on either side of the valley. Vines start to appear, accompanied by vast cherry plantations. Approaching the Loire valley, below the Gâtinais, the Puisaye area extends as far as Nièvre. In this land of sand and clay, lakes mingle with forests and hedgerows chequer the landscape. In this woodland region, isolated houses and distances are swallowed up by the vegetation. La Puisaye (pronounced Pweezay) seems to have been touched by the hand of a fairy, that of Colette, the French novelist who

Above
The Terre-Pleine area from Montréal (Yonne).

Below
The Chablis vineyard in Fleys.

was born here. She describes it with great sensitivity: "And if you came to my country on a summer's day, at the bottom of a garden that I know, a dark, leafy, flowerless garden, if you saw, in the distance, a round mountain turning blue where the stones, butterflies and thistles mingle with the same mauve and dusty azure, you would forget me...". La Puisaye has kept alive its ochre pottery tradition. Further south, the Avallonnais is a gateway to the lively contours of the Morvan range. This is Vézelay, referred to by French poet and dramatist Paul Claudel as "a boat that has cast its anchor over the horizon".

Leaving Pays d'Othe, now easily accessible from the A5 motorway, and travelling south along the border with Champagne, the plateaux give way to the Chablis hills, which are covered with vines along both banks of the little Serein river, whose name, meaning "serene", seems fitting. White stone again predominates, continuing in the style of the Langres plateau. After this comes the Tonnerrois, dry limestone plateaux where vines have been successfully replanted.

Above
Stags in the forest.
Photo R. Charpentier.

Below
The Cousin Valley in Moulin-Cadoux.

Côte-d'Or

The Châtillonnais is on the border with Champagne. It also features vines but especially large plateaux planted with bright yellow rapeseed and forests extending as far as the eye can see. A beautiful, dreamlike river with its source in the Haute-Marne flows eastward through the Vingeanne area towards the Saône. Near the ***départements*** of Haute-Saône and Jura, the region takes on the mountainous charm of Franche-Comté. Northeast of Dijon, the Tille, Ignon and Venelle form the *Pays des trois rivières*, or land of three rivers. This is where the Seine takes its source and where the first Parisian bridge can be crossed. The bridge belongs to the City of Paris, which acquired and refurbished it in the 19th century. The source is at an altitude of 1500 feet, amazingly low for such a long river.

Further south, the Auxois area is a former granary region that is now home to fertile meadows and valleys where white Charolais cattle punctuate the backdrop of green grass and clusters of trees. The Montbardois area borders the Auxois area. Its limestone spurs have long been used as refuges, citadels and lookout posts, for example Alesia, Semur-en-Auxois, Thil, Chateauneuf and Flavigny. Descending towards Hautes-Côtes and Dijon, you come to Montagne, the country of novelist Henri Vincenot (*La Bille-*

Below
The Auxois area, near Châteauneuf.

baude, Le Pape des escargots). This is a big-game region, shared by the Ouche valley, a sanctuary for hobbyist painters.

The area around Dijon is a happy medium between the limestone plateaux and the Saône plain. The area has become increasingly urbanised over the last two centuries. Canon Félix Kir, mayor of the town, had a lake built at the mouth of the Ouche valley. This greatly restricted development to the west and north (where the Order of the Golden Fleece was founded), while the east became increasingly urbanised (Quetigny, Chevigny-Saint-Sauveur and Les Tilles).

To the east, the Saône valley and plain (formerly known as the Low Country) begin in the onion fields near Auxonne and continue on to Mâcon in Saône-et-Loire. The river gradually widens, often overflowing onto the neighbouring pastureland. But still waters, as they say, run deep. The river can rise up to 26 feet, submerging everything in its wake. The waters also run high where it joins the Rhône in Lyon.

From Dijon, the Burgundy "Champs-Elysées" wine route takes

Above

Countryside close to Bruant in the Hautes-Côtes de Nuits.

Below

Pernand-Vergelesses, where Jacques Copeau (responsible for the *Nouvelle Revue Française* literary magazine and the *Vieux Colombier* theatre in Paris) gathered his *Copiaus*, or actors, and brought a new lease of life to French theatre in the 1920s and 30s.

Above
The Combe à la Vieille in Hautes-Côtes de Beaune, Bouilland.

Below
Burgundy is criss-crossed with canals, and boating holidays enable tourists to explore these villages from a different angle.

visitors to Santenay beyond Beaune. “A small, dry, ugly mountain,” wrote Stendhal, adding: “But are witty people ever truly ugly?” The narrow band of vineyards is like a ruby and diamond necklace, and each of its red and white wines is celebrated the world over, for instance Chambertin, Clos de Tart, Clos des Lambrays, Musigny, Clos de Vougeot, Romanée-Conti, Romanée, La Tâche, Grands Echézeaux, Corton, Corton-Charlemagne, Beaune, Savigny, Pommard, Volnay, Meursault, Montrachet and Santenay. Here, the cellar is the heart of every house. Stone quarries, which have supplied many Parisian monuments, including the Pyramid in the Louvre, sometimes strike a curious note, for example Comblanchien limestone, formed from coral, algae and shellfish in a shallow warm sea some 150 million years ago. In autumn, the Côte d'Or *département* is ablaze with a myriad of colours and the name Côte d'Or, or golden hillside, given during the French Revolution, fits like a glove.

Climbing towards Hautes-Côtes, a huge plateau between the Côte d'Or and the valley of the Ouche, you come across the *combes*, the steep, dry valleys of the Jura. These craggy valleys seem to have been chiselled out of the landscape. Nearby, the landscape is more reserved and hidden. Vines have taken hold, growing alongside fruit such as blackcurrant and raspberry, with the forest ever present in the background. "The sky is too near, you don't feel at home," wrote French historian Gaston Roupnel. But he was wrong as you will feel perfectly at home. The Hautes-Côtes de Nuits and Hautes-Côtes de Beaune each have their own distinctive character.

At sunrise, you can often see the Jura mountain range and sometimes even the Alps and Mont Blanc. The valley of the Saône brought clay and brick to villages such as Cîteaux, which are huddled in the ancient oak woods.

Saône-et-Loire

On the other bank of the Saône, Bresse is a marshy woodland extending as far as the Revermont in the Jura. Once entirely part of Burgundy, it was carved up (like the chicken for which it is famous) during the French Revolution, with a wing given to the Jura and half to the Ain. Its blue clay is criss-crossed with a dense network of ponds and streams. Low houses, made of brick or sometimes *pisé* (a type of clay), are surrounded by pecking poultry. *Panouilles*, or awnings for drying corn, stand in front of farms, some of which boast "Saracen" chimney stacks. Saint-Jean-de-Losne and Seurre in Côte-d'Or, and Verdun-sur-le-Doubs (at the confluence of the Doubs and the Saône), Pierre-de-Bresse and Louhans

Above
With their blue feet, white feathers and red combs, the free-range Bresse chickens are raised on grassland and boast the same colours as the French flag.

Above
The Pouilly-Fuissé vineyard under the rock of Solutré. Underneath lie some 30,000 years of archaeological history.
Below
The Morvan area, close to Saint-Léger-des-Bois.

are inviting gateways to Bresse, so different from other areas of Burgundy.

The Côte Chalonnaise is an extension of Côte d'Or and Hautes-Côtes de Beaune. This winemaking area runs from Chalon-sur-Saône and Tournus to the heart of the ***départe-ment*** and covers some twenty-five miles. Next is Les Maranges and Le Couchois. The slopes here no longer follow the Côte d'Or, but rather seem to caper and cavort along the skyline in a wide variety of forms.

Towards the Beaujolais and the Lyonnais, along the Saône, you go through Chalon-sur-Saône and then Tournus. This is where roof tiles become more curved and the region takes on the allure of the south, with its softer colours and milder climate. This is the meeting point of northern and southern Europe. Next you come to Mâcon, covered in vineyards. French poet and politician Lamartine was born and bred here (he lived in Mâcon, Milly, Monceau and Saint-Point) and he celebrated this region: "On three uneven steps of stone, fortune has rooted an ivy". This is the

start of the Beaujolais, which has just one Burgundian canton and a certain *je ne sais quoi* of sky, light and nature. Brancion, Solutré and Vergisson, rocky peaks abandoned by the limestone of the Jurassic period, seem to pin down the soil here, and houses with galleries are another type of rural architecture. Even words change from one area to the next. *Cuverie*, or fermenting room, in Côte d'Or becomes *tinailler* near Mâcon and *cuvage* in Beaujolais.

Driving west, Val Lamartine leads to Cluny, the Charolais and the Brionnais. Each village church bears witness to the splendour of Romanesque architecture in verdant countryside where delightful calves stand on their matchstick legs, already dreaming of victory in the agricultural show in Paris. The area around Blanzy is an abiding souvenir of the coal mining era. Le Creusot was the capital of an industrial empire born in the 19th

Above

The Charolais area, close to La Clayette.

Below

The Brionnais area, close to Semur-en-Brionnais.

The national stud farm in Cluny (Saône-et-Loire)

Founded in 1806, the national stud in Cluny (Saône-et-Loire) stands on the site of a former abbey church. Whether thoroughbreds, Selles français, Anglo-Arabs, French trotters, ponies or draught horses (in particular from the Auxois and Comtois), the stallions are here from July to February. The stud farm's famous names include Bellino II (three-time winner of the Prix d'Amérique) and Quart de Vin (sire of Uccello II). There is also a harness exhibition. ■

century. The Autunois is a gateway to the Morvan range, near one of its highest peaks, Mont Beuvray (known as Bibracte at the time of the Celts and the Gauls). The huge coal tips in Autun still contain oil shale, formerly used to produce gas for lighting. The first identified uranium ore also comes from here.

Above
In the Autunois area, close to Marmagne.
Top
Hedges, a familiar sight in the Charolais countryside.

Nièvre

Apart from the cereal fields of Donziais and the flat, sandy Burgundy Sologne, the Nivernais countryside slopes gently down from the Morvan range towards the Loire, the Bazois, the foothills of the neighbouring Bourbonnais region, and the vineyards of Pouilly-sur-Loire and Sancerre on the other bank of the river. The mature forest (planted by French Minister of Finance Colbert on the orders of Louis XIV to provide ship masts) covers the plateau of Amognes and Bertrange. The meadows where young cattle are fattened have made the name of the Charolais breed, which originated in Nevers and Magny-Cours alongside Grand Prix car racing.

There is a world of difference between the valleys of the Yonne (Clamecy, near La Puisaye) – as celebrated by Claude Tillier in *Mon oncle Benjamin* and by Romain Rolland in *Colas Breugnon* – and the thatched cottages of the Morvan area, the large farms in the Bazois and the breeding of the best French steeplechasers in the south of the *département*. These regions, near the Bourbonnais and the Berry, belong to central France. They are attached to Burgundy by the Morvan range and follow the Loire. The writer Maurice Genevoix made this area his "fishing ground".

Above
Nièvre, close to Château-Chinon.

Below
Rushing waters snake through Burgundy and the start of the trout fishing season is always a major event.

Above and below
House boats and narrow boats have now taken over the canals, abandoned by the barges that used to carry grain and coal. Above, the Canal du Nivernais and below the Canal de Bourgogne.

The canals, impassive rivers

Once trade routes and now reserved for tourism, with refurbished barges and house boats, many canals criss-cross Burgundy. These impassive rivers are the perfect place to unwind while meandering from lock to lock. Travellers in more of a hurry can take the Saône and the Yonne.

The 150-mile-long Burgundy canal, which runs from the Yonne (Larocher-Migennes) to the Saône (Saint-Jean-de-Losne) via Dijon, was built in the 18th and 19th centuries. The canal from the Marne to the Saône linking Langres and Pontail-

ler-sur-Saône is 47 miles long and was built in the early 20th century. Pierre Granier-Deferre shot his film *La Veuve Couderc* starring Simone Signoret and Alain Delon at the lock and canal bridge of Cheuge in Côte-d'Or. Other places of interest include the seven Rogny locks (Yonne) on the Briare canal (1642), built to link the Loire and Seine rivers over 49 yards to compensate for a drop of 27 yards. This was the first summit level canal. The Canal du Centre (in the Charolais) dates from the late 18th century. The Canal du Nivernais, linking Auxerre on the Yonne to Decize on the Loire, was completed in 1842 and was celebrated by the novelist Hector Malot in *Sans Famille* and the writer Alphonse Daudet in *La Belle Nivernaise*.

From Saint-Symphorien on the Saône to Alsace, the canal from the Rhône to the Rhine was a dream that ended in the late 20th century.

Above and below
Saône-et-Loire has successfully launched the *Voie Verte*, or Green Trail, initiative. These trails, designed for cyclists and rollerbladers, often follow canal towpaths.

Above and below
The Morvan area at nightfall when everything takes on an orangey hue.

Morvan regional natural park

The four *départements* that comprise Burgundy share the Morvan mountain range, known to the Celts as the Black Mountain. Its limits are not precisely defined but it encompasses some 430,000 acres. Avallon, Saulieu, Autun, Luzy and Corbigny are all gateways to the park. It stretches from Avallon (Yonne) in the north to Luzy (Nièvre) in the south and from Montreuillon (Nièvre) in the east to Liernais (Côte-d'Or) in the south, and measures 50 miles by 25 miles. It became a regional natural park in 1970 and its highest peak is the Haut Folin or Bois-du-Roi, at almost 3,000 feet. This granite massif has been eroded over millions of years and is punctuated with folds and rifts, and rivers hemmed in by steep hills. It resembles a mountainous region and 60% of it is covered in woodland (with conifers gradually replacing broadleaves). It is like a pavilion roof, with water dripping from all sides. The countryside is woodland enclosed by hedgerows. The houses here are roofed in blue-grey slate that blends in with the sky.

Trade in the Morvan area was for many years focused on Paris. Firewood was taken by river in "log trains", *galvachers* and *bœutiers* (herdsmen) took their cattle to the capital and nannies were hired by rich families. Nowadays, it is a huge reservoir of fresh air for visitors seeking countryside and firmly anchored traditions. From Camille Corot to Balthus, who lived and worked for many years in the Château of Chassy near Château-Chinon, painters have often looked to the Morvan range for inspiration.

Anost (Nièvre)

This hilltop village, pronounced "anno", is one of the most picturesque in the Morvan area, where folklore and musical traditions are upheld (for instance La Fête de la Vielle in summer).

Above

The *flotteurs de bois*, or wood floaters, used to leave the Morvan area and float fire wood to Paris along the rivers or on log rafts. What an adventure! It would have made a superb Hollywood film.

Below

The Upper Morvan area, close to Arleuf.

Above
Saint-Père-sous-Vézelay.

Below
Morvan area landscapes. Saint-Léger-des-Bois and, to the right, Les Settons lake.

Château-Chinon (Nièvre)

"Small town, big name". This certainly became true when its mayor, François Mitterrand, was twice elected President of the French Republic (1981 and 1988). The Hôtel du Vieux Morvan where he used to live is an institution. Apart from the Costume museum, there is another museum that houses many items and awards received by François Mitterrand during his office. This curious, kitsch museum gives an original insight into the former Head of State.

The lakes

All the lakes are recent and artificial and were built to regulate the water supply to Paris and neighbouring villages. In their beautiful country setting, they are used for water sports, camping and picnics. The villages of Montsauche and Moux are on Les Settons lake (1858, 1,000 acres). Marigny-l'Eglise and Chastellux-sur-Cure are on Le Crescent lake (1933, 400 acres). Chaumeçon lake (1935, 333 acres) is near Lormes. Pannecière lake (1950, 1,300 acres) is to

Opposite, top
The statue of Vauban in Saint-Léger-Vauban (Yonne).

Opposite, bottom
The Maison Vauban in Saint-Léger-Vauban is devoted to the French military architect and his work.

the north of Château-Chinon. Saint-Agnan lake dates from 1968 and covers 350 acres, and Saint-Martin-de-la-Mer is on Chamboux lake (1984, 185 acres).

Quarré-les-Tombes (Yonne)

The church is surrounded by the remains of one hundred and twelve sarcophagi of unknown origin.

Saint-Brisson (Nièvre)

Morvan regional natural park visitor centre (1975) has a library of books on the Morvan area, a landscape research centre, and a museum of the French resistance in Morvan from 1940 to 1944.

Saint-Honoré-les-Bains (Nièvre)

A thermal spa since the mid-19th century, its waters were already appreciated by the Romans. Its sulphur and arsenic help clear the airways. A casino has brought new life to this large, very picturesque village, chosen by film director Louis Malle for his film *Murmur of the Heart.*

Uchon (Saône-et-Loire)

At an altitude of almost 2,300 feet, this is one of the most beautiful sites in the Morvan area. This harsh habitat is a land of woodcutters, pit sawyers and clog-makers. Fashioned between 300 and 30 million years ago, the Carnaval d'Uchon is dotted with strange shapes carved out of individual black mica rocks.

The first page of French history

Left page
The rock of Solutré stands out on the horizon.

Below
Ceramic vases in the Musée de la Civilisation Celtique (Mont Beuvray). Gallo-Roman Burgundy received much wine from Italy and Spain transported by boat along the Rhône and Saône. These vases bear marks of origin.

Prehistory in Burgundy

The earliest human traces are located in Soucy, near Sens. A 300,000-year-old encampment was discovered here in a gravel pit on the banks of a river. The early inhabitants cut up carcasses of bears, aurochs, horses and even rhinoceros and elephants. Traces of Acheulean culture can be found in caves (Azé), in valley terraces (Loire and Yonne) and in alluvial deposits (Saône). Hot and cold periods alternated during the middle Palaeolithic age (between 90,000 and 35,000 B.C.), and reindeer and mammoth were a staple in the Neanderthal diet. The Neanderthals buried their dead and lived in caves in Arcy-sur-Cure, Vergisson and Créancey in Auxois. They were also advanced in stone work (especially flint tools). The countryside was gradually occupied, except in the Morvan and Bresse areas, where there are no traces of civilisation. Genay man (from 80,000 B.C.) is the oldest Burgundian. He lived near Semur-en-Auxois.

During the Upper Palaeolithic period (from about 35,000 to 9,000 B.C.), two cold periods marked the end of the Ice Age. Burgundy became a tundra again. As the climate warmed up, primitive cattle appeared. Cro-Magnon man, a near-relative of modern man, lived in tents and caverns (in Arcy-sur-Cure) or in the open air (in

Above
The Arcy-sur-Cure caves, a major prehistory site in northern France. Poster by Julien Lacaze dating from the 1930s. Photo Burgundy Tourist Board.

Marsangy). His skills improved and he hunted with an assegai mounted on a throwing stick. Animals provided clothing and necklaces. Circa 25,000 B.C., the rock of Solutré was home to a civilisation that had remarkable skills in flint-making and the hunting of wild horses. The landscape today belongs to the Mesolithic period (8,000 to 4,000 B.C.). At this time the mild, continental climate took hold. Conifers and broadleaves flourished, as did deer and boar. Agriculture and breeding gradually developed. Wheat, barley, mutton, pork and beef were the mainstays of the villagers, whose large wooden houses demonstrate the influence of Danubian culture.

Around 3,600 B.C. at the start of the Neolithic period, new inhabitants came to Burgundy via the Rhône valley. They set up camp in Chassey in the Côte Chalonnaise, near Santenay, hence the name Chasséens. This was an advanced culture with highly developed skills, particularly in ceramics. At the end of the Neolithic period (2,500 to 1,800 B.C.), the region became a melting pot of several civilisations. The Megalithic civilisation was one of the most populous, extending over the limestone plateaux and leaving behind dolmens and gallery graves. The first copper objects then started to appear and trade with distant lands intensified.

The Bronze Age (1,800 to 750 B.C.) was when the Burgundy crossroads fully came into its own. Trade brought wealth, such as the golden bracelet weighing 2.65 lb, discovered in La Rochepot (Côte-d'Or). While a ceramic and metalwork trade developed, a structured human society, linked with the Paris basin, emerged in Auxerrois in the Yonne valley. Both had very active links with the east (Germany, Switzerland and the Alps). People from the Urnfield cultures in central Europe started arriving circa 700 B.C. They cremated their dead and had rich and varied tools, weaponry and costumes (Villethierry in the Yonne).

Arcy-sur-Cure (Yonne)

South of Yonne, these caves were inhabited by Neanderthal and Cro-Magnon man as far back as 90,000 B.C. They make up a complex net-

Above and below
The treasures uncovered in Blanot (a small village in Côte-d'Or) in 1982, now in the archaeological museum in Dijon. It is unknown whether these items, which date from 1,000 B.C., were worn by a man or woman.
Musée archéologique de Dijon.
Photos Jean-Pierre Coquéau.

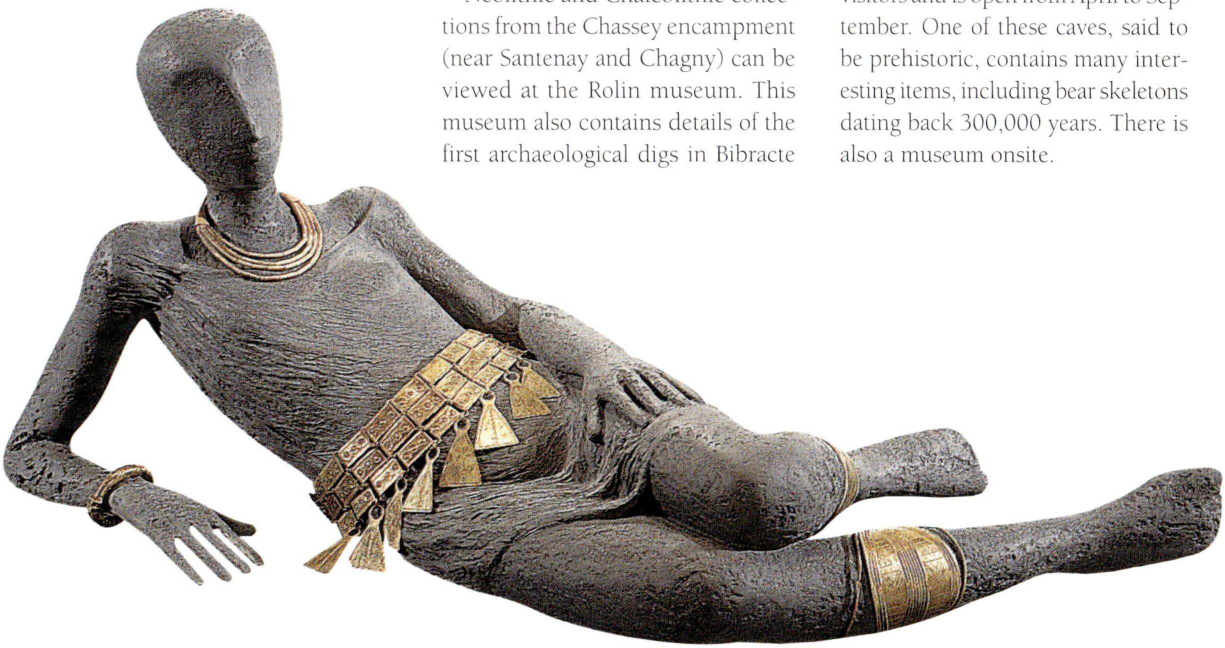

work of underground galleries. The Grotte du Cheval (featuring mammoths and horses) is the only decorated cave in Burgundy and is the southernmost one in France.

Autun (Saône-et-Loire)

Neolithic and Chalcolithic collections from the Chassey encampment (near Santenay and Chagny) can be viewed at the Rolin museum. This museum also contains details of the first archaeological digs in Bibracte on Mont Beuvray, as well as many relics of Gallo-Roman life.

Azé (Saône-et-Loire)

In the region around Cluny, the caves of Azé comprise a long network that has been specially adapted for visitors and is open from April to September. One of these caves, said to be prehistoric, contains many interesting items, including bear skeletons dating back 300,000 years. There is also a museum onsite.

Opposite
A gorgon head on the Vix vase.

Solutré (Saône-et-Loire)

In Saône-et-Loire, near Mâcon and in the middle of the Pouilly-Fuissé vineyards, the rock of Solutré stands 1,617 feet high. Lodged on a fossil-ridden limestone shelf, this rock has retained its sharp profile thanks to the extremely hard fossilised coral that has protected it from erosion. This escarpment was occupied continuously throughout the Upper Palaeolithic period. One of its cultures was called Solutrean because of the richness of the site circa 20,000 B.C. (with for example its laurel-leaf flints, sewing needles, jewellery, engravings and statuettes). Traces of a horse stampede, dating from about 23,000 B.C., can be found in magma nearby. Contrary to legend, these animals did not throw themselves off the cliff but were decimated when large herds passed through the area around Cluny and the Saône valley (Crôt du Charnier). There is a very interesting modern prehistory museum (1987), which presents Solutrean civilisation in a European context and contains exhibits from digs in Azé and Vergisson.

The Iron Age

The Iron Age ran from 750 B.C. to the Roman conquest. At this time, iron was greatly exploited and life took on new momentum. Warriors were buried underground in huge mounds complete with their swords, bronze razors, vases and other recipients. In 1954, Maurice Moisson, a farmer taking part in local digs, made the discovery of a lifetime. In Vix, in the Châtillonnais, the intact tomb of a woman aged around thirty was uncovered complete with a decorated hearse surrounded by precious objects. Among these were an exquisitely carved tiara (16 oz) and a bronze Greek vase decorated with gorgons and warriors, probably made in southern Italy circa 650 B.C. Measuring 5.4 feet high and weighing 400 lb, the vase could contain 264 gallons of wine diluted with water and it looks exactly like the vase given to Croesus as described by Herodotus.

Why Vix? In the 6th century B.C., Mont Lassois and its oppidum were

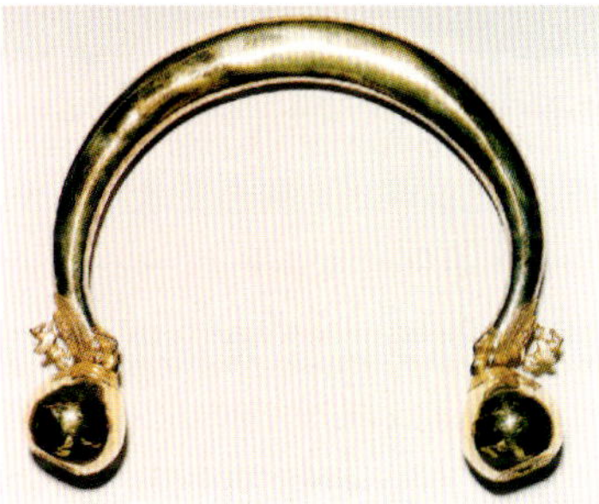

Above
Aerial view of Mont Lassois.
Musée du Châtillonnais, Châtillon-sur-Seine.
Photo René Goguey.

Opposite
The Lady of Vix's golden torc. Its origin is unknown. Some say it comes from the local area, others believe it comes from Georgia or even further a field.
Musée du Châtillonnais, Châtillon-sur-Seine.
Photo René Goguey.

Archaeological museums

Auxerre: Museum of art and history.
Chalon-sur-Saône: Denon museum (Volgu flints).
Dijon: Archaeological museum (La Rochepot bracelet, Blanot treasures, etc.).
Sens: Museum (Villethierry treasures, Marsangy digs). ■

on the tin trade route from Cornwall to the Mediterranean that passed through the Seine and the Saône valleys. There was probably a toll on this route, making this princess (or priestess?) sufficiently wealthy to source this Greek vase, the largest and finest in existence today, from over six hundred miles away. The tiara may have come from the borders of Europe and Asia. Research is still underway. In 2007, a vast chamber was discovered that may have been the palace of the enigmatic Lady of Vix.

Châtillon-sur-Seine (Côte-d'Or)

The treasures of Vix are preserved in the museum which is currently being refurbished. The treasures deserve to be displayed appropriately. If the Vase of Vix was in a small town in Greece, it would probably receive a million visitors a year! Forget the motorways and come and discover an exceptional archaeological vestige.

Dolmens and menhirs

Many of these stones are legendary and have been the subject of much geological speculation. They are evidence of the Megalithic civilisation (Ternant dolmens in Hautes-Côtes de Nuits, and menhirs from Pierre Pointe to Sussey and from Montbracon to Dommartin in the Morvan area).

Opposite
Mont Beuvray archaeological site (formerly Bibracte).

Bibracte

The first time the Gauls came together as a single nation was when almost the entire population, led by Vercingetorix, gathered at Mont Beuvray near Autun to fight Julius Caesar in Alesia. This was the beginning of French history, some fifty years B.C.

From the 5th century B.C. (the Late Iron Age, or La Tène), the region was occupied by several Celtic tribes, including the Senones (from Sens), the Lingons (from Langres), the Sequani (from Franche-Comté), the Mandubians (from Alesia) and the Eduans (from Morvan), whose capital, Bibracte, is at the summit of Mont Beuvray at an altitude of 2,600 feet. This was a vast town with a population of between 15,000 and 20,000 in an area covering 333 acres and was similar to other types of oppidum in central Europe, Hungary in particular. Craftwork and trade then developed alongside agriculture.

The Eduans allied themselves with the Romans and called on their help in 58 B.C. to repel the Helvetians. However, the wind turned. In 52 B.C., the Gauls rose up against the invader. A young Averni prince (from Auvergne), Vercingetorix, was elected in Bibracte as their leader. He made the mistake of shutting himself off in Alesia (Alise-Sainte-Reine) and, when the promised reinforcements failed to arrive, Julius Caesar laid siege. Thousands of people were trapped behind an insurmountable curtain of ditches, towers and traps. Powerless, Vercingetorix had no choice but to surrender. He was taken captive and followed the victor for several years. Caesar spent the following winter in Bibracte and it was here that he dictated his commentary on the Gallic wars, *De Bello Gallico*. Caesar then made a triumphal entry into Rome, where he had his enemy's throat cut that same evening. Gaul was dead and France had its first national hero, honoured in particular by Napoleon III.

Rome had little difficulty establishing its dominion over this land, maintaining some of its customs. Only the revolt of the Eduan Sacrovir (21 A.D.)

Opposite
Stone face, discovered in Bibracte (Pâture du Couvent) and exhibited in the *Musée de la Civilisation Celtique* at the foot of Mont Beuvray.
© Bibracte. Photo Antoine Mailler.

momentarily threatened this stability. The uprising was quickly quashed. The *Sanctuaire des sources de la Seine* archaeological museum has many wood and stone ex-voto made by local craftsmen, which were offered to the goddess Sequana to solicit healing or to give thanks. A gold object shows Sequana on her boat. Gallic culture therefore remained popular and rooted in the depths of the forest for many years. It is not known, however, how the Gauls were able to determine the exact source of the river Seine and distinguish it from the source of the Yonne.

In Mirebeau (Côte-d'Or), digs have revealed the permanent encampment of a Roman legion, illustrating the characteristics of military life.

The Romans built communication routes and the current motorway from Lyon to Trèves runs along the original Roman roadway. Augustodunum (present-day Autun) replaced Bibracte as capital, the latter being difficult to access and too closely linked to Eduan freedom. The town became "a sister town to Rome". Urban planning followed the Roman model, with a theatre, stadium and monumental gates, and the surrounding area, which was devoted to agriculture, was dotted with Roman villas. Latin became the language of religion. Autun drew wealthy youths from all over Gaul to its schools. Gods from the Mediterranean and the Orient alike were worshipped (Mithra in Bolards and Nuits-Saint-Georges, and Isis and Osiris in Autun). Christianity was introduced in the 2nd

Opposite
In the *Musée de la Civilisation Celtique* – founded by François Mitterrand who was long mayor of Château-Chinon – a reconstitution of a bronze-smith's workshop at Porte du Rebout.
© Bibracte. Photo Antoine Mailler.

century A.D. by immigrants from Greece or Syria – there is an inscription by an early Christian, Pectorios, in Autun. Vines, which possibly predate the Roman conquest, prospered thereafter. They came from the south, probably Italy.

The Pax Romana did not last long. In the 3rd century, civil war and Germanic invasions brought turmoil and terror. Every large town was under threat and therefore *castrums* were built to provide protection. During the 4th century, Christianity extended its influence. The first Burgundy saints (Bénigne, Reine, Andoche, Symphorien and Lazare) date from this time. Bishops were appointed to Autun, Auxerre, Sens and Langres and, later, Dijon. Modelled on the ancient Gallic system, this system remained in place until the 18th century.

Alesia (Alise-Sainte-Reine, Côte-d'Or)

The exact siting of Alesia was long disputed. Some said the siege took place in Guillon (Yonne), some said it was Alaise, Salins-les-Bains or La Chaux-des-Crotenay in Franche-Comté, while still others said it was Alès in the Gard or Aluze in

Above
Aimé Millet's statue of Vercingetorix (1865), commissioned by Napoleon III. It measures 23 feet in height and stands on a base designed by architect Viollet-le-Duc. This was how the Gallic chief was imagined in the 19th century.
Opposite
Bust of a young Gallo-Roman woman (1st century A.D.) discovered in Alesia.
Musée d' Alise-Sainte-Reine.

Saône-et-Loire. Digs carried out onsite, combined with aerial archaeology put paid to all this conjecturing: the siege took place in Alise-Sainte-Reine. Napoleon III, who had a keen interest in the event, commissioned a 23-foot-high copper and iron statue of Vercingetorix from Aimé Millet in 1865, and erected it on a granite plinth designed by architect Viollet-le-Duc. This chieftain epitomised Gallic man in the 19th century. There are remains of the Gallo-Roman town dating from the 1st to 4th centuries. The site is being gradually protected. Following thirty years of research, the regional authorities of Côte-d'Or will soon open a museum, and have commissioned architect Bernard Tschumi to build it. It is expected to open in 2010. It is high time that this national site had its own museum.

Above

Alésia Interpretation Centre
The Côte-d'Or local authorities have succeeded in bringing history to life here with a little help from famous architect Bernard Tchumi.

© Arnaud 25

Opposite

Mother goddess discovered in Alesia.

Musée d'Alise-Sainte-Reine.

Above Autun has retained two of four gates from the ancient town. Porte d'Arroux, which has never been rebuilt, dates from when the town was founded. Porte Saint-André (pictured) has been restored several times and is similar in design. Its outstanding watchtower now attracts numerous visitors.

Autun (Saône-et-Loire)

This Gallo-Roman town, built under the Emperor Augustus (Augustodunum), was completed at the end of the 1st century A.D. to replace the Gallic town of Bibracte on the summit of Mont Beuvray. For some two hundred centuries, this town was renowned for its university and was a melting pot of Gauls and Romans.

It contained fifty-four circular towers (now destroyed), four monumental gates (two of which – Arroux and Saint-André – still stand), the largest theatre in Gaul (which could house twenty thousand

Above Autun's ancient theatre, dating from the second half of the 1st century A.D., could hold up to 20,000 people. It was partly restored in the 1930s.

spectators and has been partially restored), the amphitheatre, razed in the 18th century, the temple of Janus (an imaginary name given to the impressive ruins of a Romanised Gallic sanctuary) and nearby monuments – such as an arena or theatre, an amphitheatre, temples and thermal baths – that have not yet been uncovered. Nearby is the pyramid of Couhard, a funeral monument from the ancient town (1st century A.D.), standing almost 100 feet high on a square base. No-one knows its purpose for sure. For many years, it was the focus of esoteric beliefs. The Rolin museum contains many souvenirs of Bibracte and Augustodunum, including mosaics, crockery and religious objects.

Mont Beuvray and ancient Bibracte (Nièvre)

This huge summit stands at an altitude of 2,625 feet, close to metal deposits and is easily accessible from the Saône, the Loire and the Seine. It was easy to defend and was occupied as early as the Neolithic period. It was the capital of the Eduans.

This long-forgotten town, abandoned in favour of Autun after the Roman conquest, was rediscovered and excavated in the 19th century. Since 1986, contemporary archaeological methods have been used by various researchers, most notably Spanish and Hungarian. These researchers have demonstrated the similarity of oppida culture throughout Europe, based more on economics than on military strength. The site, with its twisted beech trees, is superb and boasts magnificent views. Excavations have resulted in many interesting finds and there is a reconstruction near Porte du Rebout. It is also a legendary site, containing the Stone of the Wivre, from where Vercingetorix is reputed to have harangued the Gauls. Other interesting features

Above
The Temple of Janus in Autun. The remains of a larger sanctuary, set near an amphitheatre or arena and other monuments that have yet to be uncovered. The temple is loosely named after the Roman god Janus.

Opposite
The top of Mont Beuvray.

Opposite
Bronze ex-voto discovered in Dijon.

Below
Wooden and stone ex-votos from the *Sources de la Seine* site, a shrine to the goddess Sequana.

Musée archéologique de Dijon.

Photos from the museum.

Archaeological sites

Escolives-Sainte-Camille (Yonne). Champallement-Compierre (Nièvre). In Pierre-Perthuis near Vézelay, Fontaines Salées (Gallo-Roman baths, religious enclosure). ■

include the monumental basin and the horse park. François Mitterrand founded a major archaeology museum at the foot of the mountain and this modern museum recreates the civilisations of this period rather than presenting excavated objects.

Dijon archaeological museum (Côte-d'Or)

The museum has displays of ex-votos made of wood and stone from the Gallo-Roman *Sources de la Seine* shrine (dedicated to the goddess Sequana) and the *Têtes de Chorey*, gigantic human heads made of stone from a temple in Chorey-lès-Beaune of which nothing is known.

Musée de Nuits-Saint-Georges (Côte-d'Or)

This museum houses the finds of excavations carried out in Les Bolards, a very important Gallo-Roman site.

Above

A replica of a statue by François Jouffroy (1865). This nymph – symbolising the Seine – lies in an artificial cave on the site of one of the sources of the river. This feature was the work of Napoleon III and Baron Haussmann.

Les sources de la Seine (Côte-d'Or)

Saint-Germain-Source-Seine near Saint-Seine-l'Abbaye (Côte-d'Or) is the most likely site of the main source of the Seine and was acquired in the 19th century by the City of Paris, which built a false grotto and a statue of the goddess Sequana in the style of Jouffroy here. The site was known as far back as Celtic times. It was like the Lourdes of its day in a way. People came here from afar to be healed or to offer their thanks to Sequana. Hundreds of anatomical parts (an arm, an oesophagus, etc.) from ex-votos of wood and stone were found in the workshop of a local craftsman in the 20th century. Naturally preserved in water for twenty centuries, they suffered damage when they came in contact with the open air. This is the largest collection of Gallo-Roman ex-votos alongside that in Chamlières (Puy-de-Dôme), also discovered in the 1960s.

The Romanesque legacy

Cluny and Cîteaux were like two candles lit in Burgundy that illuminated all Christianity for a thousand years. Here, the spirit and faith of the Romanesque legacy attains its true beauty. These abbeys, sharing the same faith, provide two successive and different approaches to the monastic vocation.

Left page
Abbey of Fontenay, one of the first monuments to be World Heritage-listed by UNESCO (1981).

Below
The dance of death and the *Dit des trois morts et des trois vifs* in the church of La Ferté-Loupière in Yonne. These rare murals date from the late 15th century.

Burgundy's identity was forged during the troubled Merovingian, Carolingian and Capetian periods. The brief passage of the Burgundians gave this region its name, along with a sophisticated legal system. Saint Clotilda came from this line of Burgundian kings. She converted her husband, Clovis I, King of the Franks, to Christianity. Later, Lotharingia (Lorraine) came under the German Empire following the carve-up of Charlemagne's realm.

Burgundy, however, chose its own path, that of Romanesque culture. A bastion against chaos and misery, the Church became increasingly strong. In the towns, the bishops were of growing importance. For example, Saint German of Auxerre (early 5th century), was a great administrator as well as a man of religion, having commanded Roman garrisons along the Atlantic coast.

Christianity took over from the ancient Gallic and Gallo-Roman belief systems, which did not, however, disappear completely. Many Christian shrines, saints, animals and characters adorning the churches are Celtic in origin. Saint-Seine, for example, succeeded the goddess Sequana. In the 5th century, Moutiers-Saint-Jean (Côte-d'Or) witnessed a new form of religious life: the monastery and the abbey. After the Council of Autun in 670, these abbeys were generally Benedictine in towns (Saint-Etienne in Nevers, Saint-Germain in Auxerre, Saint-Bénigne in Dijon, and Saint-Marcel in Chalon-sur-Saône) and throughout the countryside (Saint-Seine, Bèze and Flavigny in Côte-d'Or).

Above
Detail of a sculpture in the upper room of the *farinier*, or miller's building, in the former abbey of Cluny.

Above
In Cluny, the small bell tower and *Eau-Bénite* bell tower (12th century) crown the preserved part of the former abbey church. The small bell tower used to hold the town clock and this explains why it is still present today.

Cluny, the centre of the world

In 909 or 910, Duke William of Aquitaine gave his villa and lands in Cluny in the Mâconnais area to the monk Berno to found a monastery that would be autonomous from any power other than the pope's. Soon, Cluny became the centre of the Christian world along with Rome. The great founding abbots were Odo, Aymer, Maiolus (who turned down the pontificate), Odilo (who established the famous truce of God and instigated the commemoration of the faithful departed – All Souls' Day – the day after All Saints' Day), Saint Hugh (the great founder of monasteries) and Peter the Venerable, who sheltered Peter Abelard and reconciled him with the Church and who commissioned the first Latin translation of the Koran.

The black monks, as French historian Georges Duby described them, were a powerful, tightly-knit force imbued with team spirit. Cluny adapted the Benedictine rule for its own purposes. At its apogee (13th century), the order featured ten thousand monks in a thousand monasteries, most of them in Europe. It had real spiritual power and Pope Callixtus II was elected in Cluny. It could house up to two thousand guests and its worldly empire was limitless. "Wherever the wind blows, Cluny takes its due" says an old proverb. Cluny unashamedly covered itself in riches. After all, should God not be worshipped with the best of

Opposite
Cellar vaulting in the lower room of the *farinier,* in the former abbey of Cluny.

Below
The former abbey is now a national industrial art and design school.

everything? The divine office was held at every hour of the day and night. The abbey grew to such an extent that Cluny III (from 1080), was the largest church in Christianity after Saint Peter's in Rome. Already in decline with only forty-six monks, the order, which had been previously ruled from afar by Cardinals Richelieu and Mazarin, disappeared in 1790 with the French Revolution. The abbey was largely vandalised and destroyed in the early 19th century.

The remains of the ancient abbey, which in 1867 was converted into a national art and design school, are worth a visit, particularly for the composite façade, its 18th-century cloister, the small bell tower, the bell tower known as Eau-Bénite, or holy water, (12th century) and the southern arm of the transept. The *farinier* building (14th century) evokes the ancient abbey and boasts happily preserved capitals (Adam and Eve in particular), supported by a fabulous wooden frame. Also worth a look are Tour du Moulin (12th century), Place de l'Abbaye and Tour des Fromages (11th century base), and the stables of Saint Hugh (11th century). The Ochier museum, restored in 1992, details the rich history of Cluny.

Above
Basilica of Sacré-Cœur in Paray-le-Monial.

Ancient abbey of Saint-Germain in Auxerre (Yonne)

A major figure in the 5th century, Saint Germain was bishop of Auxerre, among many other spiritual and temporal missions. A community of monks watches over his tomb. The Benedictine abbey of Saint-Germain has been in existence since the early Middle Ages. It was a veritable university, training some two thousand students every year from all over the Christian world. There were as many as six hundred monks here. The abbey was rebuilt in the 9th century. Of this period, there remain crypts spread over two floors. They are some of the earliest relics of pre-Romanesque architecture in Burgundy (the frescoes are a complex, fascinating ensemble). The church was built in stages from the 11th century. Tour Saint-Jean was built in the mid-12th century and the current building was built between the 13th and 15th centuries. The abbey was closed during the French Revolution. Today, there is a museum

Opposite
Capital decorating the chapter room in the former abbey of Saint-Germain in Auxerre.

Above
Christ painted on the ceiling of the basilica of Paray-le-Monial. It dates from after the church was built and was discovered in 1935.

detailing the life and works of Saint-Germain.

Church of Notre-Dame in La Charité-sur-Loire (Nièvre)

The influence of Cluny spread throughout Burgundy, as far as the church of Saint-Aignan in Gevrey-Chambertin. In 1059, the first Cluniac priory was built at La Charité-sur-Loire in Nièvre on the pilgrim route to Compostela (designated a UNESCO World Heritage site in 1998). Cluny's influence also extended across Europe, as far as England, Portugal, Venice and Constantinople, up until the French Revolution in 1789. *Charité*, or charity, was called out by those who came looking for bread and aid. La Charité, coveted by Catholics and Protestants alike, had a troubled history. The buildings were dismantled and sold off but some interesting ruins remain. The church of Notre-Dame, which retains part of the Romanesque abbey church, stands among later additions from the 14th and 16th centuries.

Basilica of Sacré-Cœur in Paray-le-Monial (Saône-et-Loire)

Modelled on the architecture of Cluny and a high point of Romanesque architecture, the basilica of Sacré-Cœur was built in the late 11th century and has been restored several times since. Recent restoration work led to the discovery of an ancient building, a wonder of harmony. The ambulatory is reminiscent of the beautiful ambulatory in Cluny that was known as the "angels' walkway" but is now long gone. Nowadays a pilgrimage destination (the Emmanuel community is present here today) dedicated to the Sacred Heart (Saint Mary-Margaret), Paray-le-Monial was visited by Pope John Paul II in 1986. The museum of Hiéron, now restored, houses the Romanesque tympanum from the ancient priory of Anzy-le-Duc, near Paray-le-Monial.

Above
Detail of a portal, cathedral of Saint-Lazare in Autun.

Opposite
'The Temptation of Eve', bas-relief attributed to Gislebertus.

Top right
Bell tower on the cathedral of Saint-Lazare in Autun.

Cathedral of Saint-Lazare in Autun (Saône-et-Loire)

The cathedral of Saint-Lazare opens onto a tympanum depicting the Last Judgment, a masterpiece of Romanesque architecture (c. 1135), carved by one of the rare craftsmen from this time to have left his name: Gislebert. Built in the 12th century in the spirit of Cluny, the interior of this church has remained intact and it boasts many fine capitals. Ascending towards the chapter house, you will see other capitals on the transept and chancel. The capital portraying the Magi being woken by an angel, who shows them the star at their bedside, is rightly famous. However, you will need to go to the Rolin museum to admire the capital of Eve, which formerly adorned the lintel of the tympanum over the north portal. Discovered by chance in the stonework of a house, Eve is naked and half-lying on the ground, casually stretching out her arm behind her to take hold of the apple, the forbidden fruit, the image of a woman who is already human. This marks the high point of Romanesque sculpture. It would be wonderful to see Adam, who is most likely still hidden in the stonework of some nearby house.

Above
St. Madeleine in Vézelay.

Below
The chevet, St. Madeleine in Vézelay.

Basilica of St. Madeleine in Vézelay (Yonne)

The basilica of St. Madeleine, perched atop a hill, is not a monument but an act of faith. The relics of Saint Mary Magdalene have been kept here since the 10th century. They are probably fake but nevertheless her devotees erected a powerful abbey in her honour. The church, built in the 12th century and restored in the 19th century by Viollet-le-Duc, looks a little like a ship run

Above

Unique in Romanesque architecture, the great tympanum of the narthex in Vézelay where John the Baptist presents the Mystery of the Church. The apostolic mission is represented by far-off or mythical figures.

Above

One of the capitals in Vézelay representing beekeepers.

aground, inhabited by grace. It is an exceptional example of Romanesque architecture (possibly the work of Gislebert of Autun). The great tympanum shows an impassive Christ in Glory – his legs seem to be moving and his robe is swirling around him. The apostles are receiving their evangelical mission and you have to look closely to see which far-off people are described here by the Romanesque imagination – Byzantine perhaps? The architect designed the church to be flooded with sunlight at the time of the solstices. The alternating white and greenish-grey stones of the transverse arches in the nave are unique in Burgundy – they are reminiscent of Spanish architecture although no-one knows why. The ninety-nine capitals take their inspiration from the Bible and sometimes from Celtic legends. Light is to Vézelay what honey is to sugar. Vézelay was a necessary stop on the route to Compostela, the place

where Saint Bernard of Clairvaux preached the Second Crusade. It remains a beautiful site conducive to meditation and was World Heritage-listed by UNESCO in 1979 and 2007.

Church of Saint-Philibert in Tournus (Saône-et-Loire)

A sanctuary for the Noirmoutier monks, driven back by the Viking invaders, Tournus was given a monastery very early on, which later became a rich abbey. Dedicated to a local saint, Saint Philibert, the recently restored abbey church was built in successive stages from the early Middle Ages on (the present building dates from the 11th and 12th centuries). The fortress-like exterior dates from the year 1000 and is influenced by Italian and Catalonian architecture (so-called Lombardy arcatures). With its pre-Romanesque crypt and upper chapel as large as a church, the ensemble expresses an architectural originality specific to Burgundy. It is the gateway to Romanesque architecture in this region. The monks' former calefactory is now a lapidary museum. The moving cloister gallery and cloister, the chapter room, the great caves and cellar, and the monks' refectory are all worth a visit. The building houses an international centre for Romanesque studies.

Opposite
The façade of the basilica of Vézelay.

Below
The nave of the former abbey church of the Tournus monks. Climb the small staircase to the surprisingly large upper chapel.

Above
Church of Saint-Etienne in Nevers.

Above
Detail of the tympanum on the church of Saint-Julien-de-Jonzy in Brionnais.

Church of Saint-Etienne in Nevers (Nièvre)

Built at the end of the 11th century by Cluniac monks, the church of Saint-Etienne in Nevers was probably built on the site of a nunnery founded circa 610 by an Irish monk, Saint Columba. The pure lines of the building reflect the influence of Romanesque Burgundy and Auvergne.

Churches in Brionnais (Saône-et-Loire)

In the south of Burgundy lies the Brionnais, where meadows are interspersed with a few forests, offering a superb panorama of rural Romanesque churches. Cluny and Paray-le-Monial are very close nearby. The same craftsmen worked here and in neighbouring Charlieu. The three-storey, eight-sided bell tower of Anzy-le-Duc is almost Tuscan, made of ochre-coloured stone. The images on the capitals deserve particular attention. Still in Anzy-le-Duc, look out for the acrobat fighting off two monsters. Although these images were long seen as Homeric or sacred texts, could these fantastic heads and strange symbolism not also be inspired by Celtic tradition? Look at the lintel of Montceaux-l'Etoile, with Christ ascending to Heaven watched by people who would have preferred him to stay with them. See the Last Supper on the tympanum of Saint-Julien-de-Jonzy. See also the archer and griffin in Varennes-

Above
The very high octagonal bell tower on the church of Anzy-le-Duc in the Brionnais area. It is almost Lombard in style.

Opposite
Gislebert's Eve in the *Musée Rolin* in Autun.

Opposite
Tympanum on the church of Semur-en-Brionnais. Rejected by the other bishops at the Council of Selecia, (359), Saint Hilaire, seated on the left on a child's chair, is called to the place of honour by an angel.

l'Arconce and read the story of Saint Hilaire in Semur-en-Brionnais. The churches of Iguerande and Châteauneuf (11th and 12th centuries) and the natural scenery has changed little over the centuries. After the year 1000, Burgundy was covered with a "white coat of churches" as described by the monk Raoul Glaber in his chronicle of that time.

Below The church of Semur-en-Brionnais.

Above
For the ninth centenary of the abbey of Cîteaux (1998), the 13th- to 16th-century library was fully restored. It is now open to visitors.

Charlieu

Charlieu is located in the *départe-ment* of the Loire and is therefore not strictly speaking in Burgundy. It is, however, very close to the Cluniac style. Its 11th-century cloister and ruins have plenty to tell about all periods of Romanesque architecture in Burgundy.

Asquins

In the valley of the Cure (Avallonnais, Yonne), the church of Asquins, though overlooked by guidebooks, was listed as a UNESCO World Heritage site in 1998. It is on the route to Compostela and pilgrims on their way to or from Vézelay once stopped here.

The towering majesty of Cîteaux

Although architecture was always devoted to the glory of God, a revolution took place in the 12th century. Like in Cluny, Burgundy was again the cradle for what was to become the birthplace of the Cistercian order, Cîteaux.

Its founder, Saint Robert, established a new Benedictine reform and he also founded the abbey of Molesmes in the Châtillonais in the 11th century. In 1098, he was given marshy land in the Low Contry (between the Côte-d'Or and the Seine valley) where he decided to establish his "New Monastery". Working in extremely harsh conditions, a handful of monks set to work building Cîteaux, the name of which comes from a small flowering shrub, the cistus.

Through poverty, austerity, prayer and work, its founders produced some of the finest manuscripts of the 12th century within the space of a few years. The richness of their illustrations shows that these artist monks were not afraid to take inspiration from the daily life of their time (grape pickers, wood-cutters and hunters). 1112 was a decisive year for the fortunes of Cîteaux, when the future Saint Bernard, born in Fontaine near Dijon, chose to enter monastic life here, accompanied by around twenty young relatives and local noblemen. The white monks threw the Christian world into disarray, as the black

Above
The exterior of the former library, abbey of Cîteaux.

monks of Cluny had done previously.

Within a few decades, from the 12th century on, Cîteaux was the mother house to 343 abbeys and, at its peak, there were up to 762 monasteries engaged in the same spiritual quest, from Scotland to the Holy Land and from Portugal to Lithuania. Saint Bernard de Clairvaux played a very important part in this history. He was the man of the century. He poured scorn on Cluny, fought with Abélard who, he held, was guilty of 'reasoning', denounced Rome, launched the crusades, preached against the Cathars, advised the political authorities, drew vocations, founded many abbeys (including Clairvaux, which he built himself, and of which he was the abbot) and left behind extensive writings as befits a Doctor of the Church.

The ascetic message of Cîteaux was translated into the bare stone seen today in many abbeys throughout Europe, including that of Fontenay in Burgundy. Tympanums and capitals no longer disrupt the view or reflection and no more stories are told. There are only a few plant motifs. This sparseness profoundly marked the Christian world. The centuries passed, temporal power took hold and the original rule was relaxed. The Order survived however, with Trappists and Trappistines now under the Order of the Reformed Cistercians of the Strict Observance (in France, La Trappe, Aiguebelle, Sept-Fons, Tamié and Mont-des-Cats). The general abbot of the order is in Rome while the head of the order is in Cîteaux. The monks on the island of Lérins are a particular branch, that of the Cistercians of Common Observance, which has sister congregations in many countries. In March 1998, the abbey celebrated its ninth centenary with abbesses and abbots from all over the world coming to Cîteaux (315 monasteries and convents from both branches of the order were represented by four thousand monks and three thousand nuns).

Abbey of Cîteaux (Côte-d'Or)

Located between Dijon and Seurre, the abbey of Notre-Dame de Cîteaux was destroyed during the French Revolution. There were many changes in the 18th century. The church and cemetery housing the tombs of the Capetian Dukes of Burgundy were destroyed, a monumental wing was rebuilt on a huge square around a bell tower that was never completed, a handful of buildings were preserved and many of its treasures were pillaged (12th-century manuscripts in Dijon municipal library, and the tomb of Philippe Pot in the Louvre). The famous Clos de Vougeot vineyard was in Cisterican hands for seven centuries. Cîteaux became in turn a factory, a phalanstery and a "penal settlement" for young delinquents. When the Cistercians returned to France in 1815, they did not forget their mother house. Thanks to a pious donation, they returned here in 1898 and are still here today, offering hospitality and discretion.

In recent years, the site has become more visitor-friendly, with modern accommodation for retreatants, a tour for visitors that includes the 13th- to 15th-century library (admirably restored in time for the ninth centenary celebrations), the *définitoire* or novices' room, a souvenir shop with many Cistercian products, including the famous Cîteaux cheese made by the monks from the milk of the abbey's own cows, and an information centre on Cistercian studies. The main attraction is the church, rebuilt in 1998 on the foundations of a 19th-century chapel. The community, comprising around forty monks (they no longer distinguish between white, brown or lay monks) assembles here for its daily offices, the first at four in the morning.

Abbey of La Ferté (Saône-et-Loire)

La Ferté, the first daughter abbey of Cîteaux, founded in 1113 near Chalon-sur-Saône, was destroyed during the French Revolution. It still has its abbot's house, a monumental building dating from the 17th and 18th centuries.

Abbey of Pontigny (Yonne)

Pontigny, the second daughter abbey of Cîteaux, founded in 1114 near Chablis, grew rapidly to four hundred monks and lay monks. The oldest buildings date from the 12th century. Several figures from British history and from Canterbury stayed here, often in exile, including Thomas à Beckett, Stephen Langton and Saint Edmund of Abbington. The abbey was destroyed during the French Revolution. From 1905 to 1940, Paul Desjardins organised famous meetings of the intellectual élite here with André Gide, André Malraux, T.S. Eliot and Thomas Mann, among others. The Burgundy Regional Council purchased the outbuildings, which remain unused. The dimensions and the quality of the Cistercian architecture of the abbey church are spectacular.

Below
The church of the abbey of Cîteaux, rebuilt in 1998 on the foundations of a 19th-century chapel.

Abbey of Fontenay (Côte-d'Or)

The abbey of Fontenay, daughter abbey to Clairvaux and founded in 1118 in the Montbardois by Saint Bernard, is listed as a UNESCO World Heritage site (1981 and 2007). The site, buildings and spirit of Fontenay form the oldest vestige of the Cistercian order and remain almost intact today. Maintained and admirably restored by the Aynard family, Fontenay lost its monks during the French Revolution but retained all its features, including the church, cloister, dormitory, chapter house, forge (12th century), prior's lodging (17th century), fountain, freshwater pond and gardens, which all radiate peace. Nestled in the depths of a small valley, this abbey at the end of the world ("bout du monde" as they say in Burgundy) guards it privacy while recalling the

Above
The cloister, abbey of Fontenay.

Top
The church of the abbey of Fontenay expresses Cistercian simplicity. It broke with the earlier tympanums and lintels that were decorated with figures and scenes.

virtues of silence and the simplicity of light playing on its stones. Jean-Paul Rappeneau shot the end of his film *Cyrano de Bergerac* here.

Other Cistercian sites

Château Clos de Vougeot (Côte d'Or) is mentioned later in the chapter on vineyards and wine. Nearby, Gilly-lès-Cîteaux is now a hotel (17th-century buildings, formerly a country residence for the abbots of Cîteaux, 15th-century Gothic cellar and 14th-century church). The cellar of Petit Pontigny in Chablis (Yonne), attached to the abbey of Pontigny (12th century), has been refurbished to showcase vintage wines. In Dijon, the cellar of Clairvaux in the town centre dates from the early 13th century, marking the beginnings of primitive Cistercian Gothic architecture.

Above and opposite
The abbey church and statue of the Virgin in Fontenay. When asked "What is God?", St. Bernard replied "He is length, width, height and depth." His architecture was inspired by this, as only depth comes from divine intuition and the sacred.

The rise of Burgundy Gothic

Religious architecture moved towards the Gothic. However, Gothic architecture did not appear at the same time throughout Burgundy. The Cistercians used ribbed vaulting in the abbey church of Pontigny as early as the mid-12th century. The chancel in Vézelay also dates from the early Gothic period. Buildings were often rebuilt in part or in full using composite additions. In the northwest of the region, the cathedrals of Sens and Auxerre are a unique expression of the majestic buildings of Champagne and Ile-de-France, both for their façades and the size of their naves.

Gothic architecture developed from the 13th century on, generally in the towns, and it was often influenced by the architecture of Champagne. Buildings were not overly large but always elegant (Semur-en-Auxois, Clamecy). Their originality is sometimes surprising (Notre-Dame in Dijon). Smaller towns and villages (Saint-Seine-l'Abbaye, Saint-Père-sous-Vézelay and Varzy) have fine churches that date from this time and some of them still retain the capacity to amaze (such as the cathedral chancel which appeared suddenly in Saint-Thibault in the Auxois countryside). The abbey church of Saint-Bénigne in Dijon marks a development of the late 13th and early 14th centuries. It was designed for a monastery and is, therefore, less richly decorated but is the size of a future cathedral.

Opposite

The pier of the central portal on the cathedral of Sens is decorated with a statue of St. Stephen. It survived the French Revolution as it was disguised with a Phrygian cap.

Left page

Cathedral of Saint-Etienne in Sens.

Cathedral of Saint-Etienne and the synod house in Sens (Yonne)

The first of the great Gothic cathedrals, the cathedral of Saint-Etienne was built from the 12th to the 16th centuries. The impressive façade dates from the later period while the interior dates from as early as 1130. It illustrates the evolution of this architectural movement, culminating in the flamboyant Gothic transept dating from circa 1500. The cathedral of Saint-Etienne greatly influenced many buildings from Jerusalem to Canterbury. A contemporary of the cathedral of Saint-Denis near Paris, it is markedly different to that building. The sculpted décor was damaged during the French Revolution but retains features of particular interest, including the mediaeval central portal (early 13th century), which features symbols and representations of the liberal arts.

The former archbishops' palace complements the cathedral. It comprises the synod house (c. 1235), the officiality court comprising the ecclesiastical court and prison, the synod room, the Francis I and Henry II wings, the renovated museum and the treasure house.

Above and opposite
Portal and stained glass window of the Good Samaritan (12th century), cathedral of Sens.

Above
Cathedral of Saint-Etienne in Auxerre. The southern bell tower was never built.

Cathedral of Saint-Etienne in Auxerre (Yonne)

The current Gothic building was built on the site of a Romanesque building in the mid-13th century, traces of which can still be seen in the remarkable triple-nave crypt with a unique fresco of Christ on horseback. The proportions of the church are not huge but are in perfect harmony. The church underwent many alterations and refurbishments. The 13th- and 14th-century sculptures evoke mythological and biblical scenes, with Hercules standing alongside Adam and Eve. The chancel (c. 1230) is a wonderful example of Gothic architecture. The treasure house and collection of stained-glass windows are of exceptional quality, on a par with those of Bourges and Chartres.

Clamecy (Nièvre)

Restored during the 19th century by Viollet-le-Duc, the collegiate church of Saint-Martin (13th century) offers a rich sculpted décor and its thirty-two scenes portraying the life of the saint are of particular interest. The flamboyant style is apparent throughout the church.

Varzy (Nièvre)

The church of Saint-Pierre was completed in 1280 and is an early example of Gothic architecture extending to the Nivernais. It has an interesting collection of reliquaries.

Montréal-sur-Serein (Yonne)

This picturesque village has a church (formerly a collegiate church), which was restored by Viollet-le-Duc and which expresses the simplicity of early Gothic architecture. Sculpted in oak by the Rigolley brothers in 1526, the stalls are of exceptional interest with scenes from the Bible and daily life in the 16th century.

Saint-Seine-l'Abbaye (Côte-d'Or)

This church is an example of early Burgundy Gothic architecture and was originally part of a Benedictine monastery (built c. 1235 with later additions). The famous Burgundy snail can be seen on the portal. The décor is also noteworthy.

Saint-Père-sous-Vézelay (Yonne)

Burgundy Gothic finds a new expression here. The spire and sculptures representing the virtues and vices date from the early 13th century, as does the pediment, which, according to writer and Inspector General of French Monuments Prosper Mérimée, "replicates the beauty of the pediment in Vézelay in miniature". It depicts Christ and St. Stephen, the Virgin and St. Peter, and Mary Magdalene and St. Paul.

Saint-Thibault (Côte-d'Or)

Noticed by Mérimée in the 19th century, this church in Auxois remains a mystery. It is located in the Auxois countryside and has the apse of a great Gothic cathedral appended to a modest nave with a bell tower that was added later. The four floors of the chevet, restored by Viollet-le-Duc, soar skywards. The décor is extremely rich.

Above and opposite
The church of Saint-Père-sous-Vézelay. This tower dates from the early 13th century. According to Prosper Mćrimóo, "tho pediment replicates the beauty of the pediment of Vézelay in miniature". It depicts Christ and St. Stephen in the centre, the Virgin and St. Peter on one side, Mary Magdalene and St. Paul on the other, and other apostles.

Unspoilt Noyers-sur-Serein

In the south of Yonne, some distance away from the major roads, Noyers-sur-Serein (known as Noyère) is a wonderful little town that has remained unchanged. With its half-timbered houses and arcades dating from the 15th and 16th centuries, late Gothic-early Renaissance church, gate, roadside cross and ramparts, it is a delight to wander through. The town is a mixture of architecture from all periods up until the 18th century. Even the *lavoir,* or wash house, is a monument dedicated to domestic cleanliness. If you want to get off the beaten track and away from the major tourist sites, this secret part of Burgundy is the place for you. ■

Above
Place de la Petite-Etape-aux-Vins and Rue du Poids-du-Roy. Two very picturesque spots in Noyers-sur-Serein (Yonne). The town also features many 15th- and 16th-century houses.

Opposite
The church of Notre-Dame in Semur-en-Auxois.

Semur-en-Auxois (Côte-d'Or)

The slender church of Notre-Dame, begun in 1225, recalls the three ages of the Gothic period. Initially a priory church, and then a collegiate church, it finally became a parish church.

The epic story of the Dukes of Burgundy

The 14th and 15th centuries in Europe were the high point of Burgundian architecture and a civilisation that revolved around the great Dukes of Burgundy. The Order of the Golden Fleece is the symbol of this age.

Left page
The roofs of the Hôtel-Dieu in Beaune. The bright colours are reminiscent of the vines in autumn.

Below
The tombs of Philip the Bold and John the Fearless (*Musée des Beaux-Arts* in Dijon).

The death of the young Duke of Burgundy Philip I of Rouvres from the plague in 1361 at the age of 19 marked the end of the long line of the Capetian duchy, which spanned three centuries. It was a dark moment in the history of the region. The country was ravaged by bands of mercenaries known as *Grandes Compagnies* and by

Above
The *Palais des Ducs et des Etats de Bourgogne*, or Palace of the States General of Burgundy, in Dijon.

epidemics. With no direct heir, the duchy was successfully claimed by the King of France, John II the Good, who, in 1363, handed it down to his son, who earned the nickname Philip the Bold after winning the disastrous Battle of Poitiers. According to legend, he valiantly assisted John the Good, crying "Father, watch out to the left! Father, watch out to the right!"

The first of four Valois Dukes of Burgundy, Philip the Bold married the fiancée of Philip of Rouvres, the richest heiress on the continent, Margaret of Flanders. Upon the death of his father-in-law in 1384, he inherited the County of Burgundy (now Franche-Comté), the Nivernais, Rethel, Artois and Flanders. At the time, Flanders was an important economic and trading centre. For a century, the Dukes of Burgundy revelled in their power as this was the height of their territorial, political and cultural influence.

A dream of a State

John the Fearless succeeded his father in 1404. He tried to dominate France and in doing so covered his hands in blood. He was assassinated on the bridge of Montereau in 1419 by a blow to the head: "it was by this hole that the English entered France". His son, Philip the Good, who was much wiser, led the duchy until 1467. From his mother, Margaret of Bavaria, he inherited Hainaut, Holland and Zealand, and from his cousin Saint-Pol he inherited Brabant, Limburg and Luxembourg. The power of the Burgundy Dukes was at its height. Allied with the English, Philip the Good fought the Dauphin of France. Burgundy thus fought Armagnac and Joan of Arc fell victim to them. Eventually embracing the French cause, Philip the Good won Bar-sur-Seine, Auxerre and Mâcon in exchange for his allegiance.

His son, Charles the Bold, pursued this policy of Burgundian independence from 1467 until his death in 1477. He tried, unsuccessfully, to persuade the emperor to crown him king of Burgundy in Trier. He attempted to seize Lorraine and Alsace. Defeated by the Swiss in Grandson and Morat, he was killed at the Battle of Nancy.

From 1364 to 1477, the four Valois Dukes gradually built up a state between the empire and the kingdom. Known as Lotharingia, it was an old dream of one of Charlemagne's sons. They were doubtless encouraged by the riches and power of their dominions: Flanders, Hainaut, Brabant, Luxembourg and Artois. Through this singular historical adventure, the Dukes of Burgundy were equally at home in Brussels, Malines, Bruges, Ghent and Antwerp, even more so than in Beaune and Dijon. The dukes spoke Flemish and treated their capital Dijon like a sort of family home. This was where they were born and brought up. This was where they were buried. This was their granary, their cellar. While the dukes eagerly pillaged and ransacked everything in their wake, irritated by the rising sentiment for public liberties in Flanders, here they played at being patrons of the arts.

The idea of Burgundy

Extending from the slopes of the Jura mountains to the polders of Friesland, from the vineyards of Mâcon to the dunes of den Helder, from the quays of the Saône to those of Antwerp, and from the mists of the Rhône to those of Zealand, Burgundy lived out a dream that sometimes overwhelmed it and that it never fully understood. It did not speak up when Charles the Bold (who spent only one week here in his entire life) publicly called for "a kingdom of Burgundy long usurped by the kings of France" in Dijon, echoing the loss of Lotharingia, six hundred years previously. The idea of Burgundy was finally laid to rest in the church of Notre-Dame in Bruges, where the body of Mary of Burgundy lies beside that of her father, Charles the Bold. She married Maximilian of Austria and died young. Upon her death, her husband inherited Franche-Comté, Artois and the Netherlands. With Charles V, this inheritance became Austrian, French and Spanish.

Louis XI brought Burgundy under the French crown. There was no more talk of a "free Burgundy" – apart from a Nazi propaganda plot during the Second World War. The legacy of the Idea of Burgundy is the progressive march towards continental unity, often mentioned by Archduke Otto, head of the house of Habsburg-Lorraine, a descendant of Mary of Burgundy and an advocate for Europe in the 20th century. The Burgundy of Philip the Good has now effectively been united in an entangled web of nations, cultures, languages and mutual respect.

Above
Decoration on the *Palais des Ducs et des Etats de Bourgogne.*

Below
Staircase in the *Palais des Etats* in Dijon. The work of Jacques Gabriel, premier architect of France (1733-1738).

Above
The statue of Philip the Good by Henri Bouchard (c. 1930) in *Square des Ducs* garden behind the Hôtel de Ville, Dijon.
Opposite
The tower of Philip the Good (1443) reminds the States of Burgundy what they owe to the Great Dukes of the West.

The Order of the Golden Fleece

The Order of the Golden Fleece was founded on 10 January 1430 in Bruges by Philip the Good on the occasion of his wedding to Isabella of Portugal. Along with the Order of the Garter, it is one of the sole orders of knighthood still in existence today. The original ethos was as much religious as political: members of the nobility from all corners of Burgundy pledged an oath of allegiance. Jason, the man who betrayed Medea can hardly be called a Christian hero but a minor character

The mourning procession on the tombs of the Dukes of Burgundy (*Musée des Beaux-Arts* in Dijon).

Opposite
The Jacquemart clock. It was seized from Kortrijk by Philip the Bold in 1382 and given to Dijon. A wife and two children were later added. Church of Notre-Dame.

from the Bible, Gideon, was found to fit the bill. Initially there were 24 knights, then 30, then 50.

The order was transferred by Mary of Burgundy to the house of Habsburg. It gradually came under Spanish control. When Charles II died without an heir in 1700, the order was claimed by the new King of Spain, Philip V, founder of the Bourbon dynasty of Spain, and by the Habsburgs in Austria. Right up to modern times, it has been the principal order of knighthood in Spain and has sometimes been awarded to non-Catholic sovereigns, such as Emperor Hiro-Hito, King Hussein of Jordan and Queen Elizabeth II of England, by King Juan Carlos I with the approval of the government. Archduke Charles of Habsburg-Lorraine, son of Archduke Otto, became head and sovereign of the so-called Austrian Order in 2002. It has members in many European countries, has retained the original cross on which the oath is taken and is faithful to the founding principles of the order. It met in Dijon on Saint Andrew's Day in 2007 for the first time since 1433. Unfortunately, the order's seat, the Holy Chapel, was demolished in the early 19th century to make room for the museum of fine arts.

Dijon, the museum of Europe

The Valois Dukes were wealthy patrons and they and their entourage played host to great artists. Claus Sluter from Haarlem and his successors, Claus de Werve, Antoine Le Moiturier and Juan de La Huerta from Aragon gave rise to the Burgundy school of sculpture. Philip the Bold founded the charterhouse of Champmol in Dijon to house the tombs of the ducal family. The recently restored Well of the Prophets, still in place, is a masterpiece of universal sculpture. The prophet's only equal was Michelangelo. The tombs of Philip the Bold and John the Fearless, surrounded by a mourning procession of altar boys and monks, are now to be found in the fine arts museum in Dijon among many other works from this period, including some by the Master of Flémalle, Robert Campin.

Dijon has many souvenirs of the great ducal period, for example the ducal kitchens (1433), the tower of Philip the Good (1433) in the ducal palace, and houses from the same period including Hôtel Chambellan, Hôtel Thomas Berbisey, Hôtel Morel-Sauvegrain and Maison Millière.

Above
The Well of the Prophets, sculpted by Claus Sluter.
Photo Emmanuel Pain.

Opposite
The Virgin and Child from the former charterhouse of Champmol. It is attributed to Claus Sluter (late 14th century).

Germolles

Near Chalon-sur-Saône, the Château of Germolles was a favoured residence of Philip the Bold and especially his wife Margaret of Flanders, who created a model vineyard and rose garden whose crops were used to make perfumes in Brussels. Claus Sluter worked on decorating this ducal residence.

Nevers

The first of all the châteaux of the Loire and the nearest to the source of the river is in Nevers. Construction began in 1464 by Jean de Clamecy, Count of Nevers and nephew to John the Fearless. It continued until 1565, adapting to changes in taste up until the Renaissance. Two famous families are connected with the history of the château: the literary Clèves and the Gonzagues, who gave Poland two queens.

Scattered masterpieces

It is impossible to understand Burgundian art without visiting all of Belgium. The Vienna Kunsthistorisches Museum has items belonging to the Order of the Golden Fleece. The museum of art and history in Bern houses the "spoils of Burgundy", taken during the ill-fated Swiss wars of Charles the Bold. In the United States, the Cleveland museum has four weeping figures from the ducal tombs, the Baltimore museum has one of the sides of the tomb of Pierre de Bauffremont, Harvard University has a Gothic ceiling from Dijon, the Cloisters museum in New York has items from the abbey of Moutiers-Saint-Jean, the Philadelphia museum has items from the chapel of Pagny-le-Château and, of course, the Louvre houses the tomb of Philippe Pot. ■

Above
Gilded wooden altarpiece from the charterhouse of Champmol (1391) by Jacques de Baerze.
Musée des Beaux-Arts in Dijon.

Left page
Courtyard of the Hôtel-Dieu in Beaune.

Above
The *Salle des Pôvres* in the Hôtel-Dieu in Beaune.

The Hospices of Beaune

Surrounded by its ramparts and bastions, like staves around a barrel, Beaune is the only town in the world where, as the architect Viollet-le-Duc once said, you actually would not mind falling sick.

An advisor to John the Fearless and later chancellor to Philip the Good, Nicolas Rolin had an immense fortune. After hesitating between Autun, his native town, and Beaune, he founded a hospital here in 1443, giving rise to the wonderful building that, according to a Burgundy principle, has a showy roof. Visitors will be dazzled when they enter the courtyard. The oriental design suggests the colours of the vine in autumn and the sun in mid-winter. How could you forget the wife of chancellor Rolin, Guigone de Salins? In the *Hôtel-Dieu*, or general hospital, the word "Seulle" (meaning 'alone') is often encountered. Was this a testament to Guigone's fidelity? A cry of passion from Nicolas?

No monument better summarises the love affair with Flanders at the time of the great dukes and during the cultural exchanges and civil and charitable work. The *Hôtel-Dieu* may have been built by Jacques Wiscrere and based on Saint-Jacques hospital in Valenciennes, which has now disappeared. It was completed in 1451. The first nuns came from Valenciennes and Saint-Omer. The community wore large wimples in the form of a church spire. You may recall the film *La Grande Vadrouille* (Tea for Two), which was set here, where Gérard Oury entrusts Bourvil and Louis de Funès

Above
The *Salle des Pôvres* in the Hôtel-Dieu in Beaune. The old and sick were cared for here, often two to a bed.

to the care of these ladies of charity during World War II. The last nun retired in 2006 over five centuries after the order first arrived here.

The *Hospices* of Beaune were formed in 1805 from the *Hôtel-Dieu* and the *hospice* of La Charité. Together, they formed a considerable demesne, particularly in terms of vines donated over the centuries and farmed directly by the order. The annual wine auction on the third Sunday of November is a global event now overseen by Christie's. It helps promote the heritage of the *hospices* and the new hospital, founded on another site in 1971.

Looking at the entrance canopy, the façade dominated by slate and the bell tower from where the *trézeleur* rings out the bells, you cannot imagine the roof and courtyard inside, home to one of the largest early music festivals. The tiles were replaced several times during the 20th century according to designs of previous buildings. We have no idea whether the original roof looked anything like this.

The great hall or *Chambre des Pôvres* (234 feet by 45 feet) has not been used since 1946. The wooden beds, with their red curtains, the painted beams and the polychrome wooden Christ de Pitié (an original feature from the 15th century) all bear witness to how the sick and old were cared for over the centuries, often two to a bed. At the back of the hall, near the altar, once stood the polyptych of the Last Judgment, which has been housed in a purpose-built room since 1975. Variously attributed to Van Eyck and Memling, it has now been attributed with certainty to Rogier Van der Weyden (Roger de la Pasture), an artist of the school of Robert Campin, the Master of Flémalle, and official painter to the Burgundy court at the time. We know that this major work was painted in Brussels circa 1445 for this specific place. The altarpiece has been in place since the *Hôtel-Dieu* was founded. Housed in the Louvre since 1874, both sides can be viewed at once because the frame has been cut. Treated like a tympanum, the main scene shows St. Michael weighing the souls. His look expresses the absolute detachment of justice, between Heaven and Hell. Nicolas Rolin (whose portrait by Van Eyck also hangs in the Louvre) and Guigone de Salins are on the reverse.

Right page
St. Michael weighing the souls during the Last Judgment. Polyptych by Rogier Van der Weyden for the Hôtel-Dieu in Beaune (c. 1445).

Above
Tapestries of the Life of the Virgin, Collegiate Church of Notre-Dame in Beaune (Tournai, late 15th century).
Below
Basilica of Notre-Dame in Beaune.

Some rooms were refitted during the 17th and 18th centuries. There are also many tapestries from Tournai and Brussels (15th and 16th centuries). The *pharmacie* contains pottery from Nevers. Do not miss the kitchen and famous Maître Bertrand, an automatic roasting spit.

Basilica of Notre-Dame in Beaune

This collegiate church, built from the 12th century on for the canons of Beaune, is reminiscent of the church of Saint-Lazare in Autun. The tapestries of the Life of the Virgin most likely come from Tournai (late 15th century) and may be the work of the artist Pierre Spicre.

Above
The palace of the Dukes of Burgundy in Beaune. Today it houses a museum devoted to Burgundy wine.
Top
Château de La Rochepot in the Hautes-Côtes de Beaune. It was almost entirely rebuilt in the early 20th century.

Palace of the Dukes of Burgundy in Beaune

This beautiful and vast stately home was built from the 14th to the 16th centuries and, as was frequently the case, it became a royal residence. The first museum dedicated to Burgundy wine and wine-making was opened here in 1946 by Georges-Henri Rivière, the first in a long line of museums devoted to popular crafts and traditions.

Château of La Rochepot

Régnier Pot, chamberlain to Philip the Bold, one of the first knights of the Golden Fleece, started building this castle on the road between Beaune and Autun in the 12th century. The work was continued by his son Jacques and grandson Philippe, right-hand man to Charles the Bold. Lodged high on a rock, this castle, with its glazed tiles, is the classical image of Burgundy, almost entirely rebuilt by the son of former French President Sadi Carnot in 1926.

The Rolin museum in Autun

The Nativity by Jean Hey (the Master of Moulins) shows Cardinal Rolin as one of the donors (1480). Along with 'Eve' by Romanesque sculptor Gislebertus, this is the major work in this stately home, much of the layout of which is due to Nicolas Rolin and his family.

A thousand and one castles dating back over a thousand years

Initially a means of defence but later a symbol of wealth and architectural progress, strongholds, fortresses, châteaux and manor houses have adorned the landscape of Burgundy for over a thousand years. They date from all periods and embrace all kinds of styles. They were often rebuilt over the centuries and are the expression of a structured social life that was very different from religious or lay history in the towns. Burgundy provides a full panoply: it is like a book of pictures that you can leaf through, going off the beaten track to discover a wealth of hidden treasures.

Left page
Château de Posanges at the gates to the Auxois area in Côte-d'Or.

Below
Berzé-le-Châtel to the northwest of Mâcon.

Above Château d'Epoisses, where the Marquise de Sévigné felt at home.

The first strongholds

The first strongholds were towers of wood and later of stone, built during the 7th and 8th centuries. They were places of refuge during these troubled times. As Françoise Vignier has written, these strongholds were residences, seats of authority, agricultural centres and safe havens during invasions. However, the picture changes slightly from one part of Burgundy to another, depending on who was in power.

These houses were usually built on a height inside an enclosure that was easy to defend – sometimes inside several enclosures, depending on the rank of the man to be protected. These were the first castles of the early Middle Ages.

Berzé-le-Châtel (Saône-et-Loire)

This fortified enclosure in the Mâconnais dates from Carolingian times. The only trace of the initial building is what is thought to have been a chapel. Although rebuilt and partially demolished many times over the centuries, the building still retains its original glory. Nearby is Berzé-la-Ville, a major Cluniac site decorated with splendid frescoes dating from the 12th century.

Brancion (Saône-et-Loire)

On the road from the Saône (Tournugeois) to Cluny, this fortress with a square keep has had a turbulent history. Perched up high, it was a pocket of resistance of the Catholic League against the royal power. This ancient, very picturesque village also has a wonderful Romanesque church.

Epoisses (Côte-d'Or)

In Auxois, the Château of Epoisses, rebuilt and altered several times, has retained the volume of a large fortified enclosure, which was destroyed during the 18th century. The castle was a silent witness to the entire political history of Burgundy and its literary golden age. The Marquise de Sévigné stayed here and much of her correspondence is to be found here. Michel de Saint-Pierre

located his highly successful novel *Les Aristocrates* here.

Mont-Saint-Jean (Côte-d'Or)

Standing high on a rocky ledge, this massive fortress of Auxois is a system of successive enclosures around three courtyards, including that of the church. Its construction was interrupted during the 16th century. The complex remained uninhabited for many years.

Semur-en-Brionnais (Saône-et-Loire)

The oldest Burgundy castle is in the Brionnais. This peak has been occupied and constantly fortified since prehistoric times. Recaptured many times between the 9th and 15th centuries, the building has retained its imposing keep and its postern, flanked by two towers. Saint Hugh, abbot of Cluny, was born here.

Above

Semur-en-Brionnais prides itself on having the oldest Burgundian castle.

Below

Château de Mont-Saint-Jean.

Above Chateauneuf-en-Auxois, which features a replica of the tomb of Philippe Pot (the original is in the Louvre).

Feudalism and its fortified castles (12th and 13th centuries)

Feudal castles were simpler and less often built on a height, sometimes without a keep and with walls that were generally quadrangular to withstand the modest weaponry of the time.

Chateauneuf-en-Auxois (Côte-d'Or)

In Chateauneuf-en-Auxois, the village and mediaeval castle bear the memory of Philippe Pot. There is an identical replica of his tomb (which was found in Cîteaux but later moved to the Louvre).

Druyes-les-Belles-Fontaines (Yonne)

Between Auxois and Avallonnais, this castle with four towers is a typical four-sided fortified castle. Deserted and rebuilt in the 14th century by Philip the Bold (notably the gate tower and its machicolations), it was once again deserted.

Ratilly (Yonne)

This 12th-century complex in Puisaye with a turbulent history has been faithfully rebuilt. Jansenists fleeing the abbey of Port-Royal took refuge here in the 17th century. During the second half of the 20th century, the Pierlot family turned it into a very active centre for contemporary art.

Fortified castles come down from the hills (14th and 15th centuries)

The art of warfare evolved with the invention of gun powder and artillery. The lords began to consider comfort a little more and built more practical dwellings on lower ground with huge farm buildings. There were fewer towers but well-defended keeps. They had immense stone chimneys, spiral staircases and sometimes a single tower surrounded by ditches.

Right page
Château de Ratilly in Puisaye.

Above
The surprising fortified castle of Chevenon.

Below left
Château de La Motte-Josserand.

Below right
The impressive Rosières keep.

Chevenon (Nièvre)

Built in the 14th century by Guillaume de Chevenon (a captain of the tower of Vincennes who took inspiration from that building), this quadrangular castle keep, flanked with round corner towers, is one of the most impressive in the Nivernais area. Writer George Sand loved this place and was instrumental in saving it during the 19th century.

Commarin (Côte-d'Or)

This 12th-century stronghold was transformed in the 15th century by a chamberlain to Philip the Bold who later became commander of the artillery under John the Fearless. The huge enclosure and castle were rebuilt many times over the centuries. It is one of the rare castles that has been in the same family since the 12th century (Vienne, Damas, Vogüé). It has a rich décor of wall tapestries. The Burgundy writer Henri Vincenot lived in Commarin. He recounts his memoirs in *La Billebaude*.

La Motte-Josserand (Nièvre)

This late 14th-century quadrangular castle in Donziais is a typical example of fortified buildings of the time.

Posanges (Côte-d'Or)

Just outside Auxois on the Dijon road, this castle was built circa 1440 and restored in the 20th century. The view of the exterior is splendid. It is a rectangular construction with thick corner towers and a drawbridge. It was carefully restored in the 20th century by a wine merchant from Beaune but remains closed to the public.

Rosières (Côte-d'Or)

Rosières, dating from 1321, on the border between Burgundy and Franche-Comté, is a perfect illustration of the revival of the large keep. It has painted décors dating from the late 17th century and a magnificent main building that has been faithfully restored.

Above

The Château de Commarin in the Auxois area. Its 16th-century tapestries feature coats of arms with symbols and mottos, fire balls and hunting scenes.

Above
Château de Bussy-Rabutin in the Montbardois area. It was made famous by its memoir-writer owner in the 17th century.

The early Renaissance

Bussy-Rabutin (Côte-d'Or)

This tough fortress near Montbard was made famous by Roger de Bussy-Rabutin, a 17th-century libertine and writer of memoirs, who lived here for many years and decorated it to his tastes. It owes much to the 16th century and was remodelled in the Italian style. Now fully restored, the castle gives a glimpse of the intrigues and love affairs of the court of Versailles, through paintings commissioned by Bussy-Rabutin during his exile from Paris.

Chailly-sur-Armançon (Côte-d'Or)

On the edge of Auxois, this castle, whose floor plan is reminiscent of the ducal palace in Nevers, dates from the first half of the 16th century. Abandoned for many years, Chailly is now a sumptuous Japanese-funded hotel and restaurant near a golf course.

Fleurigny in Thorigny-sur-Oreuse (Yonne)

In the Oreuse valley in the Sénonais area, this mediaeval residence was rebuilt in the 16th century in the Burgundy Renaissance style. In the 19th century, it was restored in the English style that was so popular at the time.

Above and opposite
Roger de Rabutin, Comte de Bussy, a notorious memoir writer during the reign of Louis XIV. The décor in the golden tower includes portraits of key figures from the court of Versailles together with juicy details, and mythical figures.

Nevers (ducal palace)

Several families rebuilt this palace between 1464 and 1565 (the Clamecy, Clèves and Gonzague families). Its early Renaissance façade resembles that of a castle of the Loire. Although it retains much of its mediaeval architecture, it also has many Renaissance features, proof that there was contact with Mantua. The complex was almost completely restored in the 19th century.

The golden age of the Renaissance

Ancy-le-Franc (Yonne)

This square construction in the Avallonnais area has four wings and four corner pavilions. It was built by the Clermont-Tonnerre family between 1544 and the middle of the following century. It is thought that the architect

Above and opposite
The ducal palace of Nevers (bas-reliefs on the central tower restored in the 19th century).

Opposite and below
Outstanding painted décor and harmonious architecture in the Château d'Ancy-le-Franc.

was either Pierre Lescot or the Italian Serlio. Once past the orderly façade, you will discover a painted décor that luckily has survived, comprising the Medea, Sacrifice and Pharsale galleries, the chamber of flowers, the hall of the Caesars and a chapel. Louvois, a minister of Louis XIV, acquired Ancy-le-Franc in 1683.

Maulnes (Yonne)

In the Tonnerrois (Cruzy-le-Châtel), this lovely, enigmatic and solitary residence dates from the end of the 1560s. Antoine de Crussol, the husband of a

Above
Château de Sully in Saône-et-Loire. The home of the Mac-Mahon family.

duchess of Uzès, commissioned an unknown architect (perhaps Serlio) who used the pentagonal floor plan employed in some Italian castles, such as Caprarola near Rome. A well in the centre with five-storey-high walls has given rise to some esoteric interpretations. This abandoned and endangered masterpiece was forfeited from the State (an exceptional case), acquired and restored by the *département* of the Yonne and is now returning from the oblivion that once blighted it. Patrice Chéreau shot some of the scenes for his film *La Reine Margot* here (1994).

Sully (Saône-et-Loire)

This late Renaissance castle between Chalon-sur-Saône and Autun retains the quadrangular plan but it has angled square towers overlooking the moat. Like almost everywhere else, it was originally a mediaeval castle until Gaspard de Saulx-Tavanes, Lieutenant General of Burgundy, commissioned a new castle, built between 1573 and 1616 by an architect from Langres, Nicolas Ribonnier. It has been in the hands of the Mac-Mahon family for over two centuries (the Count of Mac-Mahon, Marshal of France and Duke of Magenta, and the first President of the Third Republic was born here in 1808). Some of it was rebuilt in the neo-Renaissance style.

Tanlay (Yonne)

Tanlay sits majestically behind its huge circular towers and freshwater moat in the Tonnerrois area. The *petit château* stands in front of the larger building like a triumphal arch. As in Ancy-le-Franc, the slate roof is reminiscent of the châteaux of the Loire valley. Built by several families (including the d'Andelot and Particelli D'Émery families) from 1550 to 1650, it is the work of Dijon architect Pierre Le Muet and possibly Bertrand de Cazenove. The entrance hall is lined with busts of the Caesars and opens onto many rooms decorated with family portraits by Philippe de Champaigne, Nattier, Mignard and Largillière, among others. The reception gallery has a trompe-l'œil

décor that was the work of Italian craftsmen. Connected to the memory of Gaspard de Coligny, Admiral of France, and the Protestant faction, the tower known as *La Ligue* was used by the School of Fontainebleau to provide an allegorical interpretation of a song by Ronsard, with the court of Henry II depicted as ancient gods and goddesses.

Opposite and below
Château de Tanlay in the Tonnerrois area.

The art of good living (17th-18th centuries)

Bazoches (Nièvre)

Rebuilt at the end of the 15th century by Antoine de Follet, chamberlain to Louis XI, this residence became famous when Marshal Vauban, who was born very near here and was ever-faithful to the Morvan area, bought it in 1675. He remodelled it and used it as a country residence and as a base for his engineering teams. The Sigalas family (who own the Château de Cheverny in the Loire valley) restored it during the 1990s and opened it to the public. It has many interesting features and Clouet and Rigaud are among the painters whose work adorns the apartments.

Cormatin (Saône-et-Loire)

Near Tournus, this castle was rebuilt circa 1610 by Antoine du Blé d'Uxelles, governor of Chalon. It evokes the memory of Alphonse de Lamartine, the writer Jacques de Lacretelle (who was born here) and

Above
Château de Bazoches, the former residence of military architect Vauban.

Raoul Gunsbourg, director of the Opera of Monte-Carlo, who entertained famous musicians and dancers here. In 1981, four friends decided to save Cormatin from ruin, restoring the "gilded apartments" (one of the richest décors from the time of Louis XIII), carrying out other interior work and remodelling the gardens and grounds. The work is still ongoing. The castle has paintings attributed to Velasquez, Nattier, Rigaud and Mignard among others.

Drée (Saône-et-Loire)

Near La Clayette to the south, the Château de Drée was built by Charles de Blanchefort de Créquy from the 1620s to the end of the 17th century. For more elegance and style, the castle was given a U shape, an advance on the square castles of the time which were protected from all sides.

Entre-Deux-Monts (Nuits-Saint-Georges, Côte-d'Or)

The solitary Entre-Deux-Monts in the hamlet of Concœur-et-Corboin in Hautes-Côtes de Nuits is an example of the style of Louis XIII. The Dijon architect Pierre Le Muet is thought to have had a part in its construction. The bossing around the doors and windows is very characteristic of this period. The Barbier family, provincial noblemen, built it circa 1650. The current owners are currently undertaking large-scale restoration work.

Below
Château de La Clayette (Saône-et-Loire).

Saint-Fargeau (Yonne)

The Duchess of Montpensier, also known as La Grande Mademoiselle, who took part in the uprising known as La Fronde and fell in love with the Duke of Lauzun, came to Saint-Fargeau in the centre of Puisaye when she was exiled from the court from 1652 to 1657 and again from 1662 to 1664.

She used her time here to rebuild the old castle, calling on Parisian architect Jean-François Le Vau, who preserved and remodelled the six bell towers and connected them via the main building. One of these was the work of Michel-Robert Le Peletier in the 18th century, whose family gave the French Revolution its first martyr, Le Peletier de Saint-Fargeau. Writer Jean d'Ormesson, whose family owned the castle in the 20th century, set his novel *Au plaisir de Dieu* here. In 1979, Saint-Fargeau was bought by brothers Michel and Jacques Guyot, who decided to return it to its former glory. They created one of the first open-air historical re-enactments with local people. The brothers are also behind the initiative to build the Guédelon fortress using only 13th-century building techniques.

Villemolin (Nièvre)

Near Corbigny, Villemolin dates from the 16th and 17th centuries and has mediaeval features, a neo-Gothic chapel and a tower added in the 19th century. The film *Le Mystère de la chambre jaune* was entirely shot on location here by Denis Podalydès (2003).

Below Château de Saint-Fargeau, which was the setting for Jean d'Ormesson's novel "Au plaisir de Dieu".

Above
The *Salle des Gardes* in the Château de Saint-Fargeau.

Pierre-de-Bresse (Saône-et-Loire)

The ecomuseum of Bresse (1980) occupies part of this castle, built in 1680 by Claude de Thyard on the site of a fortress. Its U shape is in the spirit of the time and it is flanked by round towers. The brickwork reminds us that this is Bresse, a land of clay. Nearby stands the Château de Terrans, the work of Jean-François de Truchis and Dijon architect Edme Verniquet (1765).

Vantoux (Côte-d'Or)

In Messigny-et-Vantoux near Dijon, this castle, built by Jean de Berbisy, the first president of the *Parlement* of Burgundy at the very beginning of the 18th century, is a stately country home. Its sober, square design was inspired by the architect of Louis XIV, Jules Hardouin-Mansart, who worked on the palace of the States General in Dijon. This castle, dedicated to the glory of the *Parlement* of Burgundy, is open to the public on European Heritage Days but the exterior alone is well worth the detour.

Beaumont-sur-Vingeanne (Côte-d'Or)

Another treasure, this miniature castle was built along the lines of Parisian mansions by the abbot Jolyot (1724) in the Vingeanne area, northeast of Dijon.

Montjeu (Saône-et-Loire)

The grounds of this castle cover 1,828 acres and have 10 miles of continuous walls. Set in Autunois, Montjeu is the work of President Jeannin, a significant figure during the reign of Henry IV (early 17th century). It has passed through many hands (the Le Peletier family from Saint-Fargeau, the Talleyrand-Périgord family and the Princes of Ligne) and was even owned by the late British-French financier Sir James Goldsmith. Montjeu boasts outhouses that are as fine as the master's residence.

Above
Château de Chastellux, set on a granite hillside in the Cure Valley (Yonne). It has been in the same family for nine centuries.

The châteaux of the Nobles of the Robe

Building fever originating in the court of Versailles started to flag. In the 18th century, residences were influenced by members of the *Parlement* of Burgundy, who were more prosaic and relatively discreet. Neoclassicism had arrived.

Talmay (Côte-d'Or)

Standing on the border of the Côte-d'Or and the Haute-Saône, Talmay comprises a 13th-century keep, and castle commissioned by Pierre I de Filsjean circa 1760. The architects were Jacques-Louis Daviler (Paris) and, later, Jean-Antoine Caristie (Dijon). Baron Paul Thénard set up a laboratory here to develop the use of carbon disulphide as an insecticide against the vine disease phylloxera.

Arcelot (Côte-d'Or)

Near Dijon to the east (Arceau), this neoclassical castle was designed by Philippe Verchère and Dijon architect Thomas Dumorey in the mid-18th century. Owned by the hospitable Loisy family, it is open to the public and boasts a wonderfully decorated large drawing room (*grand salon*) and vast grounds.

The neo-Gothic and neo-Renaissance in the 19th century

After the French Revolution, it was time to repair the damage. Several castles were burnt to the ground and rebuilt during this period.

Chastellux-sur-Cure (Yonne)

This castle in the Avallonnais passed back and forth between members of

Above Château de Saint-Point in the Mâconnais area where Alphonse de Lamartine did most of his writing.

one of the oldest Burgundy families from the 11th century onwards. It was completely rebuilt in the neo-Gothic style during the first half of the 19th century.

Bresse-sur-Grosne (Saône-et-Loire)

This strange castle in the Chalonnais, designed by Parisian architect Sanson circa 1870, is a curious mix of the neo-Gothic, neo-Renaissance and the neoclassical.

Saint-Point (Saône-et-Loire)

In the Mâconnais, this castle was one of Alphonse de Lamartine's favourites. He wrote much of his work here and also chose to be buried here. Keeping his memory alive, his family retained ownership until the 1990s. Saint-Point recalls the English neo-Gothic style, circa 1855, in homage to Lamartine's wife, Marianne Birch.

The last châteaux

Brochon (Côte-d'Or)

Built circa 1900, Château de Brochon near Gevrey-Chambertin was modelled on Azay-le-Rideau. A parliamentarian from the second Empire and onetime poet, Stephen Liégeard had this to say: "What Burgundy is missing, are the châteaux of the Loire." He remains famous for having inspired the story *Le Sous-Préfet aux champs* by Alphonse Daudet when he was sub-prefect in Carpentras and even more so for being the first to call the French Riviera the "Côte d'Azur".

Guédelon (Yonne): a 21st-century stronghold

In an isolated spot in La Puisaye, between Saint-Sauveur and Saint-Amand, dozens of quarrymen, stonemasons, stone cutters, woodcutters, ropemakers, carpenters, blacksmiths, tile makers, basket makers and carters are today building a stronghold. The idea was dreamt up in 1997 by Michel Guyot, who also runs the restaurant in Château de Saint-Fargeau. The aim was to build a 13th-century style fortress using only techniques and tools available at the time. It would be modelled on the nearby castles of Ratilly (Yonne) and Yèvre-le-Châtel (Loiret) dating from the time of King Philippe Auguste of France. Work began straight away and building is expected to take thirty years. Guédelon is no mere dream, it is becoming reality. The drawings were done by Jacques Moulin, head architect of the National Bureau of Historic Monuments. A team of skilled and recognised scientists oversees the site. The site is open to the public every day except Wednesday from March

Above and opposite
An ongoing project, Guédelon is being built using only mediaeval techniques. Page 97 features drawings of all the different stages planned until the completion of the castle in 2025.
Photos Guédelon

2010

2012

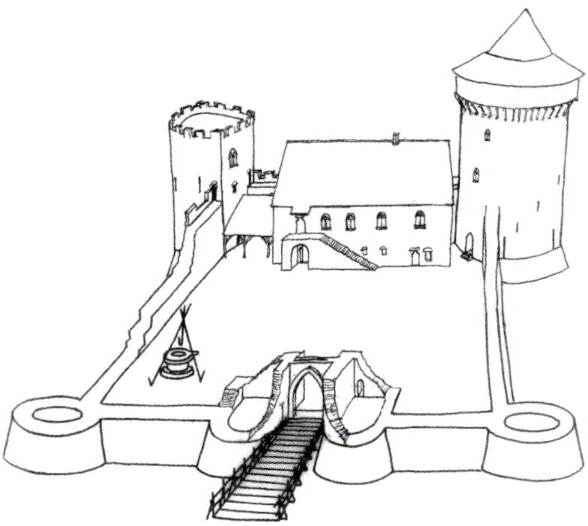

2015

2020

2025

The Guédelon building site and a model of the future castle.

Photos Guédelon. Computed-generated image: Nicolas Gasseau.

Above
The Château de Guédelon is now well above ground.

Opposite
Work is conducted exactly as in 1230, the year of reference chosen by those who dreamt up the project. This is a difficult exercise as it calls for great originality.
Photo Guédelon.

to November and daily in July and August. It is very visitor-friendly and is well above foundation level (you will see walls, towers and ribbed vaulting). There are, however, no cellars or dungeons: excavation would have taken years without much to show for it.

The initiative is mainly funded by visitors. In only a few years, Guédelon has become a major attraction as the only construction project of its kind using such restricted methods and techniques. This project was planned and mounted as a self-funding entity, although since 1997 it has received some funding from the regional council.

Above

The materials are brought by horse-drawn cart and the stone is cut onsite.

Opposite

Ribbed vaulting under construction in Guédelon.

Photo Guédelon.

Inner havens of peace

Left page and below
The abbey of Sainte-Marie de La Pierre-qui-Vire was built in several stages from 1850 to 1955 (the guest quarters welcome those seeking a religious retreat or just a period of calm).

Burgundy is a very spiritual place. The abbey of Notre-Dame de Cîteaux is still thriving and its retreat accommodation centre was restored in the early 21st century. There are also other havens of peace for visits, retreats and reflection.

Abbey of Pierre-qui-Vire (Saint-Léger-Vauban, Yonne)

Near Saint-Léger-Vauban in the Avallonnais (the birthplace of Vauban), the abbey of Sainte-Marie de La Pierre-qui-Vire stands in a beautiful granite setting. The unsteady rock, or *pierre qui vire*, that gave it its name is now held fast and topped with a statue of the Virgin to banish the fairies (it is

Above and right page The village and mediaeval site of Flavigny-sur-Ozerain.

not a dolmen). Founded in 1850 by Father Jean-Baptiste Muard, this Benedictine monastery belongs to the Subiaco congregation (Monte Cassino). It has about a hundred monks. The church dates from 1871, the monastic buildings and accommodation quarters were added later. Cheese is produced here and the abbey founded the Zodiaque publishing house, famous among others for "La Nuit des Temps" (a great collection of books on Romanesque architecture), although the printing is now done elsewhere.

Flavigny-sur-Ozerain (Côte-d'Or)

A Benedictine monastery featuring as many as 800 monks was founded in this little mediaeval town in the 8th century. Its crypts are some of the oldest vestiges of Carolingian architecture in Burgundy. The building has been partly preserved within a factory that produces aniseed, the sweet that is popular worldwide. Several religious foundations settled in Flavigny over the centuries, notably the foundation of Henry Lacordaire, who restored the Dominican order in France in the 19th century and settled here. In 1972, Maison Lacordaire became a French seminary for followers of the highly conservative Roman Catholic archbishop Lefebvre. Shortly afterwards, the former smaller diocesan seminary in Hôtel Couthier de Souhey (18th century) was occupied by the Benedictine monastery founded by Father Augustin Joly. It now has around a hundred monks, also traditionalist but firmly within the Roman Catholic fold.

Paray-le-Monial (Saône-et-Loire)

Renowned for its Romanesque architecture and also for a splendid Renaissance building, Paray-le-Monial is a holy town and birthplace of the Devotion to the Sacred Heart. The visions of Saint Margaret Mary Alacoque in the convent of the Visitation (1673-1676) were universally recognised, and she was canonised in 1920. Devotion to the Sacred Heart grew strongly in the 19th century with the Sacré-Coeur in Paris and the national pilgrimage to Paray-le-Monial. In 1986, Pope John Paul II celebrated mass in a huge field here, confirming the role of the charismatic Emmanuel community in developing religious pilgrimages here. Pilgrims here visit the chapel of the Visitation where the apparitions took place, the chaplains' park and the eucharistic museum of Hiéron, now restored.

Convent of Saint-Gildard in Nevres (Nièvre)

This is the mother house of the Sisters of Charity Order in Nevers that has two hundred houses worldwide. Sister Marie-Bernard lived in the convent of Saint-Gildard (1856) from 1866 until her death at the age of 35 in 1879. She was Bernadette Soubirous to whom the Virgin appeared in Lourdes. The Sisters of Charity founded an orphanage here. Saint Bernadette, who was canonised in 1933, lived humbly here. She is entombed behind glass inside the chapel. Hundreds of thousands of pilgrims from all five continents gather in Nevers every year in her memory. There is a

Above
The basilica of Paray-le-Monial, built between 1090 and 1110 and modelled on the abbey church of Cluny. "It tells us what Heaven is like", wrote Canon Denis Grivot, a leading specialist in Burgundian Romanesque architecture.

replica of the grotto where the apparitions took place, a museum and a souvenir shop.

The ecumenical community of Taizé (Saône-et-Loire)

The son of a Swiss Protestant pastor and a woman from Burgundy, theologian Roger Schutz founded the community of Cluny in Lausanne in 1940. In 1944, with three Swiss friends, he settled in Taizé, a small village perched on a hilltop near Cluny. This ecumenical community led by Roger, its prior, soon drew Protestants, Catholics and Anglicans. In 1953, the Rule of Taizé sealed the fate of this "springtime within the church", as John Paul II described it during a visit in 1986. In 1982, the church of the Reconciliation was built. Already in 1974, Roger Schutz had launched the youth council on the immense platform on top of the hill, attracting some 40,000 young people. The council is still held every year somewhere around the world. Taizé continues to attract innumerable young people, particularly in the summer, camping and praying together in a huge campsite. At one of these events on 16 August 2005, a disturbed young woman attacked Brother Roger, then aged 90, stabbing him. He died a few minutes later, leaving behind a universal legacy: bringing people together before the same God of peace and love.

Above The basilica of Paray-le-Monial underwent major restoration work in the late 1990s.

The Buddhist community of Kagyu Ling (La Boulaye, Saône-et-Loire)

Near Toulon-sur-Arroux in the Autunois, the Château of Plaige has, since 1974, been home to a large Buddhist centre in the tradition of Vajrayana, one of the three vehicles of Buddhism. Founded by the very venerable Kalu Rimpotche, this monastic college marks the expansion of this form of Buddhism, highly popular in Europe and America today. The community is welcoming and discreet, living happily side-by-side with the neighbouring Judeo-Christian religions. When the Dalai Lama came to Burgundy, he visited Cîteaux but not Kagyu Ling: the three vehicles have yet to implement ecumenism. This is not a sect. The deer on the gate evoke love and compassion. The wheel denotes study. It takes three years, three months and three days of uninterrupted retreat to train as a lama here. The Himalayan temple of the Thousand Buddhas is the largest in Europe and the statue of Buddha Sakyamuni measures 53 feet high. There are workshops and training courses available here that are both unusual and profound.

REGVLA CŒLVM EST
TVTVS ABIS

Beautiful towns

Left page
The astronomical clock of Auxerre (1470) which indicates both sun and moon time.

Below
The town of Autun in the heart of the Morvan countryside.

Autun (Saône-et-Loire)

The gateway to the Morvan range, Autun is a Roman and Gallo-Roman town with later Romanesque additions. (See Autun in the chapters "Prehistory in Burgundy" and "The Iron Age" and, for the cathedral of Saint-Lazare of Autun, see the chapter "The Romanesque legacy"). The curious coal tips you can see here date from the 19th-century mining of oil shale, formerly used for gas lighting.

Auxerre (Yonne)

Overlooking the Yonne meandering towards the Seine, the town is a maze of narrow, steep, winding streets and ancient monuments. The abbey of Saint-Germain and its crypts and the Gothic cathedral of Saint-Etienne are the major attractions in Auxerre but there are others. These include the clock tower in the heart of the old town (late 15th century, completely restored in 1983) which marks

Above
Place Saint-Nicolas in Auxerre.

solar and lunar time. The hands do not move at the same speed but meet at midday (new moon) and midnight (full moon). Take the time to visit the house of Cadet Roussel, a bailiff from Auxerre who inspired a famous popular song. There is a statue of him by François Brochet, who also produced a hyper-realistic statue of the poet Marie Noël. In addition to the museum of art and history in Saint-Germain, there is the Leblanc-Duvernoy museum (featuring Chinese tapestries that made Beauvais famous in the 18th century and a rich collection of china, much of which came from Auxerre) in a handsome 18th-century mansion, and the nature conservatory, which recalls the memory of scientist and politician Paul Bert, who was born in the town. AJ Auxerre, founded in 1905, also attracts crowds of football fans to its matches, held at the Abbé-Deschamps stadium.

Auxonne (Côte-d'Or, capital of Val de Saône)

Auxonne has always been a military town and now, in the early 21st century, it is one of the last garrison towns in the region and has a large Army regiment. Napoleon Bonaparte was, in fact, stationed here as a young officer. There are remains of the fortifications.

Avallon (Yonne)

Built on a hilltop above the Cousin, a small but turbulent stream, Avallon is surrounded by ramparts, towers and, luckily, gates. The warm and charming atmosphere recalls that of provincial novels of yesteryear. A statue of Vauban by Bartholdi overlooks *promenade des Terreaux*. Linked to Cluny for many years, the collegiate church of Saint-Lazare was inspired by Romanesque architecture. The museum of the Avallonnais has been renovated. It has an eclectic collection, including works by Toulouse-Lautrec, Rouault (the *Miserere*) and Jean Desprès, a major French goldsmith in the second half of the 20th century.

Beaune (Côte-d'Or)

This town features elsewhere in this book, notably for its *Hôtel-Dieu*, its atmosphere and its position as the capital of Burgundy wine. See chapters "The epic story of the Dukes of Burgundy" and "Burgundy wine".

Above
Avallon, high up in the hills.

Below left
A watchtower on Beaune's ramparts.

Below
The cloister, Notre-Dame of Beaune.

Chalon-sur-Saône (Saône-et-Loire)

Between the wines of Côte Chalonnaise and the meadows of Bresse, Chalon-sur-Saône is a thriving town on the banks of the Saône, which widens here to form the island of Saint-Laurent. Although Kodak recently shut down a major factory here, photography, which was invented here by Nicéphore Niépce in the early 19th century, still has a strong presence in this town (the Niépce museum and, not far away, the house where the first photograph in history was taken in Saint-Loup-de-Varennes). Many of the 300 million bottles of Burgundy wine are produced in Chalon (Saint-Gobain) as are nuclear reactors. The church of Saint-Pierre (circa 1700) and the cathedral of Saint-Vincent (11th to 15th centuries and neo Gothic additions) complete the visit to the recently refurbished museum of Vivant-Denon (Baron Vivant-Denon founded the Louvre museum). The quays and old streets should be explored on foot. The tower of Doyenné (15th century) has an unusual history. It was dismantled, taken to Paris and then bought by Frank Jay Gould, who rebuilt it here in 1926.

Above

The Saône river in Chalon. Though mostly calm, it can rise by 26 feet.

Charolles (Saône-et-Loire)

The county of Charolais, west of Cluny, was in turn Burgundian, Austrian and Spanish, before coming under French rule in 1684 to settle a gambling debt. Prior to this, Charles the Bold was Count of Charolais before becoming Duke of Burgundy. Besides cattle breeding (the Charolais breed originates from here) and a rich history of china production, Charolles has many old convents (Poor Clares and Visitation, 16th century) as well as the remains of a castle and its defences.

Châtillon-sur-Seine (Côte-d'Or)

Set on the border between Burgundy and Champagne, this town witnessed many wars. In 1814, the ill-fated Congress of Châtillon tried to reach agreement between Napoleon and the allied powers. In 1914, Commander-in-chief Joffre directed the Battle of the Marne from here. In 1940, 220 houses were destroyed in a bombing raid. In 1944, the French armies arriving from Normandy and Provence met in Nod-sur-Seine. The treasures of Vix, a major 20th-century archaeological discovery, make Châtillon worth a visit. The primitive 11th-century Romanesque-style church of Saint-Vorles commemorates Saint Bernard. The Douix spring is a Vauclusian resurgence with a flow of up to 660 gallons per second. It flows into the nascent Seine just over 300 yards away.

Below
The small town of Charolles.

Cosne-sur-Loire (Nièvre)

At the confluence of the Loire and the Nohain (a small river that inspired the pseudonyms of artists Franc-Nohain and Jean Nohain), Cosne's history is like that of all towns on the banks of a river. It was the site of rivalries between the Berry and the Nivernais in Burgundy, and between the bishops of Auxerre and the counts of Nevers. Looking at the pleasant, serene town today, you would never guess its turbulent history. The church of Saint-Agnan was once part of a Cluniac priory attached to La Charité-sur-Loire. Some interesting features remain. In the museum, Chagall, Derain, Dufy, Utrillo and Vlaminck proudly hold their own. Called the forges of the Vulcan by the Marquise de Sévigné, the old forges of La Chaussade witnessed considerable activity between the 17th and 19th centuries. A 2.58-ton anchor, found in the port of Rochefort in 1861 and now displayed in a square in Cosne, was forged here.

Decize (Nièvre)

This pretty town is also known as "En Loire assise". The river is calm here in the south of Nivernais. And there is so much water, including the confluence of the Aron and the Loire, the Canal du Nivernais, the confluence of the lateral canal and the Loire, and the Vieille Loire. Writer Maurice Genevoix, a native of the town, often told of fishing and hunting parties in this area far from the beaten track. The ramparts, the church of Saint-Aré, the cloister of the Minims, the gate of the marquis d'Ancre and the clock tower all bear witness to the history of the town.

Opposite
The church of Notre-Dame, located in the heart of old Dijon, nestles within the narrow mediaeval streets.

Dijon

The capital of Burgundy has modernised itself without losing its soul. Cutting-edge research and industry have grown up here alongside a Town of Art and History that is part of European heritage.

In this town, when you arrange to meet someone, it is usually at the *Coin du Miroir*, the main crossroads in the old town, which owes its name to a house that has now disappeared. A few feet away, the *Maison aux Trois Visages* witnessed the entrance of Charles the Bold into Dijon over five hundred years ago.

The Burgundy plateaux give way suddenly to the Saône plain. The town stands with its back to the hillside, with the Jura in the distance. Dijon is just the place to stop for a breather, recharge your batteries and enjoy a good meal. This town is an ancient crossroads.

Meetings of fortune

Dijon has had a fortunate history. The Dukes of Burgundy opened the town up to Europe when they chose it as their capital. It drew all the benefit of this without suffering the consequences. It has never been touched by war in all its history and so no enemy has ever destroyed it. This means that Dijon has a particularly rich heritage and is a living work of art.

Whether by chance or design, Dijon has excellent rail and road links. There are motorways in every direction and the high-speed TGV train can take you as far as London, Brussels, the south of France, Mulhouse and Switzerland on the Rhine-Rhône line. One of the first modern, welcoming town centres was built here in the 1980s, a far cry from the matchbox developments with no proper planning, far away from all amenities, in Quetigny and Chenôve. In the 1960s, a university campus was set up here for 25,000 students, at a time when there were only 3,000. Robert Poujade, who was mayor from 1971 to 2001, gave the town an auditorium worthy of the great capital cities, and the lake, created by another former mayor Canon Kir in 1964 in the face of unanimous opposition, is now appreciated by all.

Mustard, blackcurrant and *pain d'épice*, a local version of gingerbread, make this ducal city a destination for food lovers. This regional capital, with 150,000 inhabitants (230,000 in the greater urban area), is not only feted for its cuisine but also for its major automotive and pharmaceutical industries. It is a university town where research is focused on agronomics and agriculture.

The churches of Dijon

The cathedral of Saint-Bénigne was originally the church of an abbey founded in the 6th century, when Saint Bénigne is said to have converted Dijon. It was given two successive basilicas, with Romanesque additions built shortly after 1000 by William de Volpiano and of which the crypt remains. The final addition was the current church (late 13th century, early 14th century). The late 19th-century spire is 180 feet high, the tallest in France.

Saint-Philibert is an ancient church currently being restored. The main door is Romanesque and it also has some 15th-century features. The stone bell tower dates from the 16th century.

Notre-Dame was built in the early 13th century and restored in the 19th. Its originality lies in its three rows of gargoyles on the façade, which so astonished Henry Miller in *Tropic of Cancer*. The *Jacquemart* (a clock with figures) comes from Kortrijk (1382), where it adorned the belfry. The Black Virgin statue (which is actually multi-coloured) dates from the 11th century. Known as Notre-Dame- du-Bon-Espoir, or Our Lady of Good Hope, it protects Dijon and inspired writer André Malraux.

Saint-Michel has an astonishing Renaissance façade on a flamboyant Gothic building (15th and 16th centuries).

Opposite
Notre-Dame's façade with fifty gargoyles.

Saint-Jean, the mid 15th-century church where French bishop and orator Bossuet was christened, is now a theatre (Théâtre national de Bourgogne).

The chapels of Godrans, Sainte-Anne and the Carmelites are also worth a visit.

Civil architecture

The *Palais des Ducs et des États de Bourgogne*, or Palace of the States General of Burgundy, was built from the end of the 17th century until the French Revolution, on the imposing remains of the Valois dukes' palace (which included the Tour de Bar, 1365; ducal kitchens, 1433, and the tower of Philip the Good, 1443). It faces Place Royale, where the statue of Louis XIV on horseback by Jules Hardouin-Mansart once stood, and which is adorned with the work of architects from Versailles and Paris (for example the staircase by Jacques Gabriel dating from 1735, the Chapelle des Elus, the Chamber of States, and Salle de Flore).

Mediaeval houses include Hôtel Chambellan, rue des Forges; Hôtel Thomas-Berbisey, rue Berbisey (flamboyant Gothic); Maison aux Trois-Visages, rue de la Liberté; Maison Millière, rue de la Chouette; and houses in rue de la Verrerie and rue de la Chaudronnerie.

Renaissance houses include Maison Maillard, rue des Forges; Maison des Cariatides, rue de la Chaudronnerie; and Hôtel Le Compasseur, rue de la Vannerie.

Above

The church of Saint-Michel which, like a history book, presents all the orders of ancient architecture.

Opposite

Timber-framed house on Place François-Rude in Dijon. Today it is a restaurant.

Houses from the classical period include Hôtel de Vogüé, rue de la Chouette; Hôtel Bouhier de Savigny and Hôtel Legouz de Gerland, rue Vauban; Hôtel Chartraire de Montigny and Hôtel du Commandement militaire, rue de la Vannerie; Hôtel Bouhier de Lantenay, rue de la Préfecture (now the police headquarters); Hôtel Févret de Saint-Mesmin, place Bossuet; Hôtel des Barres, rue Chabot-Charny and Hôtel Fyot de Mimeure, rue Amiral-Roussin.

Dozens of old town houses dating from the 17th and 18th centuries are preserved in an area covering almost 250 acres around the *Parlement* and the States General of Burgundy.

19th-century architecture includes the theatre (from the Bourbon Restoration period), the old market, Place Darcy and Place Saint-Bernard (second half of the 19th century).

The auditorium was built in 2000 by a Franco-American team and is considered to be one of the best in Europe.

Above
Dijon theatre, built in the early 19th century.

Below
Rue de l'Amiral-Rousseau.

Opposite
Renaissance-style Hôtel Fyot de Mimeure in rue Amiral-Roussin, Dijon.

Below
Jardin Darcy, typical of late 19th-century urban planning. It draws on the underground reservoir of water that supplies Dijon.

The museums of Dijon

The *Musée des Beaux-Arts* (museum of fine arts) features the heritage of the Dukes of Burgundy (the tombs of Philip the Bold and John the Fearless with weeping figures, altarpieces by Jacques de Baerze, early Netherlandish paintings, and *Nativity* by the Master of Flémalle), large collections and the so-called Granville donation, representing artists from Georges de La Tour to Nicolas de Staël. It also houses major exhibitions in the summer.

Musée Magnin is a town house that retains the atmosphere of its previous owners, enlightened art lovers in the early 20th century. They were brother and sister, he was advisor to the court of financial auditors, she was a painter and critic.

The *Musée archéologique* (archaeological museum) in the former Benedictine abbey of Saint-Bénigne has some pieces of note, including the Blanot treasure, the bracelet of La Rochepot and statues from the sources of the Seine.

The *Musée d'Art sacré* (museum of religious art), housed in a former church built circa 1700 by the Bernardine order, has treasures of religious art from all over Côte-d'Or.

The *Musée de la Vie bourguignonne* in Perrin-de-Puycousin is housed in the buildings and cloister of an old monastery (rue Sainte-Anne). Its exhibits relate the story of Dijon and rural life in Burgundy.

The *Musée d'Histoire naturelle* (natural history museum) is an attractive, modern museum with some unique pieces, such as the Glyptodon fossil found in the Argentine Pampas.

The *Musée de Plein Air* (open-air museum) on the university campus of Montmuzard has sculptures by Arman, Agam, Karel Appel and Gottfried Honegger.

For contemporary art, go to the FRAC and the Consortium. ■

Above
Hôtel de Vogüé, rue de la Chouette in Dijon. Its roofs brighten up the skyline while its architecture recalls the early 17th century.

Parks and gardens

Parc de la Colombière, extending over 84 acres, was commissioned by the Condé family (governors of Burgundy until the French Revolution) circa 1680. It is the work of Antoine de Maerle, a pupil of Le Nôtre, and is the perfect illustration of a French-style garden. *A Little Tour In France* by Henry James ends on a bench in this park.

Jardin de l'Arquebuse has one of the richest botanical collections in the world, with 3,500 species in over 66 beds. It was founded in 1833 and also has an arboretum.

Jardin Darcy is an example of 19th-century planning in the style of Napoleon III and is in harmony with the surrounding square. *The Bear,* by François Pompon, a sculptor from Burgundy, is a replica of the work that made him famous at the *Salon d'automne* in 1922.

Square des Ducs, the former garden of Margaret of Flanders, wife of Philip the Bold, is near her former palace.

Lake Kir took many patient years to become reality. Canon Felix Kir dreamt of building this lake when he was still a young seminarian in 1895. Finally, in 1945, at the age of 69, his position as mayor of Dijon enabled him to fulfil his dream. He spent nineteen years working on the project, finishing in 1964. The monumental *Grenadier* statue (by Georges Diébelt) once stood below the Pont de l'Alma in Paris, near the *Zouave* statue, which measures rainfall in the capital.

Parc de la Combe à La Serpent covers over 800 acres of nature and former quarries. It was dreamt up by the talented André Holodynski.

Port du Canal, built in the late 18th century on the Burgundy canal, now has a small marina in a beautiful setting. It is dominated by the obelisk (1786), erected to commemorate the joining of all the seas via this canal. Gustave Eiffel was born in 1832 near the port.

Above Joigny boasts delightful old residences. Here Place du Pilori.

Joigny (Yonne)

This town stands on chalky soil on the banks of the Yonne, between Auxerre and Sens. Here you again have to climb up steep little streets to discover beautiful mediaeval houses, such as the one with the tree of Jesse, the Maison de Bois or Place du Pilori. The church of Saint-Jean was built between the 16th century and the Renaissance, and has a very beautiful interior. The church of Saint-Thibault has a statue on horseback by Juan de Juni, a famous Renaissance sculptor who was born in Joigny and who emigrated to Spain. An altar is dedicated to Saint Madeleine-Sophie Barat, who came from this parish and who founded the Society of the Sacred Heart in the early 19th century (there are now almost 600 such communities worldwide). She was canonised in 1925. *La Côte Saint-Jacques*, a restaurant run by the Lorain family, is one of the best restaurants in France.

Le Creusot (Saône-et-Loire)

The Le Creusot power-hammer, dating from 1876, was once the most powerful in the world. It was able to open a walnut without damaging the kernel. Standing 70 feet high, it has a hammering weight of 100 tons and is displayed as a public monument in this town, a symbol of 19th-century industrial development. From 1836 on, the Schneider empire grew on the site of the former "Cristaux de la Reine" factory (which dated from 1787), building locomotives, submarines, bridges, lighthouses, cannons and armour plating. It was a veritable world capital of iron and steel, a high tech factory town that constantly churned out products with engineers and design offices onsite. In 1960, the vicissitudes of the world of finance shattered the group, then called Empain. Creusot-Loire broke up in 1984. All that remains of the empire are plants here and in Chalon-sur-Saône manufacturing bogies for the high-speed TGV train, and Areva, the nuclear power company. Château de la Verrerie (which has retained two ancient furnaces) has an ecomuseum that recounts the height of industrial development in Le Creusot and this industrial heartland. It tells

the story of a town where everything belonged to Schneider.

Mâcon (Saône-et-Loire)

"Queen of the Saône" in southern Burgundy and the homeland of Alphonse de Lamartine, who was born here in 1790, Mâcon is a colourful town with painted house fronts along the quays and lining the streets up towards the upper town. Pont Saint-Laurent has straddled the river since the 11th century and it retains a venerable appearance. The people of Mâcon are very attached to the bridge and the traditional sport here is rowing, for which a special pool has been built. Built in the Regency style, Hôtel Sénecé is a centre for studies of the literary works and political activities of Lamartine. If you visit this hôtel, you will also want to visit other places marked by the writer, including Maison de Milly, Bussières, Châteaux de Monceau, Pierreclos and Saint-Point. Rarely have a town and its surrounding area remained so attached to a historical figure. The religious buildings are subdued but the Ursuline museum (a former 17th-century convent) is worth a look. The Mâconnais and neighbouring Beaujolais are famed for their wine, for their laid-back way of life similar to that in the south of France, and for their enterprising wine shows.

Above
Château du Creusot. The "Cristaux de la Reine" factory and its conical furnaces, converted into a chapel and a theatre by the Schneider family.

Below
Quai de Saône in Mâcon.

Above Near Montbard, the old Buffon ironworks.

Montbard (Côte-d'Or)

This industrial town specialising in the manufacture of pipes (notably for nuclear power) remembers French naturalist Georges-Louis Leclerc, count of Buffon. His substantial work includes extensive research on natural history, which ensured his scientific renown, and the *Jardin du Roi* in Paris, now the *Jardin des Plantes*. Attached to his town, he often lived here and developed ironworks in the nearby village that bears his name. He designed *Parc Buffon* in the mid-18th century which features a 15th-century keep, the Tour de l'Aubespin, a studio and terraces. In the early 19th century, a museum was dedicated to the memory of this illustrious figure and to that of his collaborator, Daubenton, also from this area.

Montceau-les-Mines (Saône-et-Loire)

This new town was built in 1856 in the heart of the Blanzy coal fields, which had been worked since the 16th century. These mines experienced rapid growth under the Chagot company from 1818 with over 100 mine shafts, and coal production reached 2.5 million tons per annum in 1960. In 1946, eight shafts were still open and there were 11,000 miners, many of them Polish. Near Le Creusot, in the same valley, Montceau had a different destiny hundreds of feet down – the hard life of the miners, tragedies (89 deaths in 1867 alone), social strife, the slow decline of the industry in the late 20th century with some strip mines, and the ever-present memory of a civilisation dedicated to coal. As in the south of Nièvre, there are considerable coal reserves here but they are difficult to access.

Below
Cathedral of Saint-Cyr-et-Sainte-Juliette (or Julitte) in Nevers. It was largely destroyed by bombing in 1944 and was rebuilt to feature contemporary stained glass windows.

Above
The shrine of Saint Bernadette in the convent of Saint-Gildard in Nevers. Bernadette Soubirous lived with the community of nuns in Nevers until her death.

Maybe one day… The town is pleasant and is an example of how a former mining town can come back to life by turning to other assets.

Nevers (Nièvre)

The beautiful ducal palace (from the mid-15th century to the mid-16th century) is the first château of the Loire as you go down the river. The river, swollen by the Allier, is at the heart of this town, which connects Burgundy to the Bourbonnais and Berry areas. The high 14th-century gateway tower, known as the Porte du Croux, is a relic of the ramparts. Seriously damaged by bombing in 1944, the cathedral of Saint-Cry and Sainte-Juliette, built over the course of several centuries (11th-century crypt and late 15th-century Entombment), has been faithfully rebuilt. Its stained-glass windows are the work of contemporary artists Raoul Ubac, Alberola, Gottfried Honegger and Claude Viallat. The Cluniac church of Sainte-Etienne is a meeting point of Auvergne and Burgundy Romanesque architecture. The Gonzague family from Italy contributed to the prestige of the town from 1565 to 1659. The development of china and the famous *Bleu de Nevers* (visit the Frédéric-Blandin museum for its collections of china and spun glass) date from this period. Saint Bernadette (of Lourdes) lived out her religious vocation in Nevers. She is buried in the convent of Saint-Gildard, which is now a place of pilgrimage. Alain Resnais chose this town as a backdrop to his film *Hiroshima Mon Amour*.

Above
Semur-en-Auxois, the setting for so many films.

Nuits-Saint-Georges (Côte-d'Or)

Between Dijon and Beaune, Nuits is an agricultural and trading town in the heartland of the Burgundy vineyards. It stands out for its 17th-century bell tower and 13th-century church of Saint-Symphorien. Raspberry and blackcurrant from the Hautes-Côtes are transformed into liqueurs here, like in Dijon. You can find out more about this activity in Le Cassissium, a museum dedicated to the world of the blackcurrant, while the Imaginarium will tell you all you need to know about sparkling wines. The renovated museum recounts local history, from the Gallo-Roman site of Les Bolards to the *Confrérie des Chevaliers du Tastevin* wine brotherhood, set up in 1934.

Saint-Jean-de-Losne (Côte-d'Or)

Saint-Jean-de-Losne, a former bargemen's port, is now the leading French inland river port.

Saulieu (Côte-d'Or)

A gateway to the Morvan range, this village along the RN 6 road became a destination for food lovers thanks to the prestigious French chef Alexandre Dumaine. The talented chef Bernard Loiseau took over "La Côte-d'Or" and preserved its splendour, and his wife Dominique now runs the restaurant. There are in fact many restaurants in this food-loving town. The 11th-century basilica of Saint-Andoche, with its rebuilt chancel, has fine capitals and a handsome evangelistary said to have belonged to Charlemagne, a copy of which is on display. This is the homeland of sculptor François Pompon (remembered in a small but interesting museum), whose *Polar Bear* is a masterpiece of animal art.

Semur-en-Auxois (Côte-d'Or)

This wonderful small fortified town along a tributary of the Armançon has drawn many film directors, from Yves Robert to Gene Kelly. The pink granite buildings of Semur stand proudly behind its mediaeval gates and Pont Joly (1786).

Nuits-Saint-Georges.

Above The Fosse Dionne (left) in Tonnerre. This formerly sacred spring draws water from an extensive area. A *lavoir*, or wash house, was added in 1758. The Hôtel-Dieu (right), built by Margaret of Burgundy (1295), features a *grande salle* that is on a par with the Hôtel-Dieu in Beaune.

There are several towers, including Tour de l'Orle d'Or, the top of which was once gilded. It stands 144 feet high, has walls that are 20 feet thick at the base and a long scar dating from the siege of 1589. The collegiate church of Notre-Dame (from the 13th century on) was restored by French architect Viollet-le-Duc in the 19th century. The tympanum of Porte des Bleds (14th century) tells the legend of Saint Thomas. If you come through here on 31 May, you will witness the Course de la Bague, the oldest horse race in France, dating from 1639.

Sens (Yonne)

Set inside its ancient ramparts, transformed into boulevards (or *promenades*) during the Restoration, Sens is today part of the greater Paris area. Initially a Gallic town, then Roman, at the end of the 14th century it was the capital of Grande Sénonie, which included Chartres, Orléans, Troyes, Auxerre and Paris. While this leading role diminished over time, the cathedral of Saint-Etienne and the archbishops' palace bear witness to the town's religious and political importance, particularly during the 12th and 13th centuries. There are many old houses and a covered market (1882) that is a perfect illustration of the metal architecture of the period. The monumental neo-Renaissance *Hôtel de ville* (1904), opposite the cathedral, is the expression of Republican fervour.

Seurre (Côte-d'Or)

The *Hôtel-Dieu* of Seurre (late 17th century) has a *Salle des Pauvres* or hall of the poor and a remarkable pharmacy. The memory of French bishop and orator Bossuet is kept alive in his family home. Nearby Chamblanc commemorates Anne-Marie Javouhey, the 19th-century foundress of the community of Saint Joseph of Cluny (established worldwide), who was beatified in 1950 and who is recognised for the part she played in freeing slaves in the colonies, particularly French Guiana (she was known as the mother of the blacks during her lifetime).

Tonnerre (Yonne)

Tonnerre, located between Montbard and Chablis, has small stepped streets and old residences, including Hôtel d'Uzès and the house of the Chevalier d'Eon, an eccentric diplomat who spent much of his life disguised as a woman. Of the *Hôtel-Dieu*, or hospital, founded by Margaret of Burgundy and completed in 1295, there remains the *salle des malades* or sick room, which is 300 yards long, 26 feet wide, 80 feet high and has 48,000 square feet of roofs. This room, both older and larger than the *Hôtel-Dieu* of Beaune, houses the mausoleum of Louvois, a minister to Louis XIV. The town boasts a very expressive entombment (1454) and the Fosse Dionne, once a sacred spring, which draws water from an extensive area. The *lavoir*, or wash house, was added in the 18th century. In 1979, divers managed to penetrate 1180 feet from the entrance and 200 feet down in very difficult conditions. This is one of the most spectacular natural wonders in all of Burgundy.

Modern Burgundy

The ancient province of Burgundy was divided into *départements* during the French Revolution (1791). Much later, during the 1970s and 1980s, it was organised into four *départements*: Côte-d'Or, Nièvre, Saône-et-Loire and Yonne. The former Burgundy region of Bresse was carved up between Saône-et-Loire, Ain (Rhône-Alpes) and the Jura (Franche-Comté). In 2015, Burgundy and Franche-Comté merged to create a new region which, with the addition of the Doubs, Jura, Haute-Saône and Territoire-de-Belfort départements, spans 47,784 km^2 and is home to 2.82 million inhabitants in total. The duchy and county of Burgundy share some of the same history, although the county belonged first to the Holy Roman Empire and later to Spain following the death of Charles the Bold. This lasted until the Treaty of Nijmegen in 1678, when the Kingdom of Burgundy was united with the Kingdom of France.

Left page and below
Coal is no longer mined here but mine shafts were once frequent in Saône-et-Loire and Nièvre (Epinac, Blanzy and La Machine). The industry is remembered in the *Musée de la Mine* in Blanzy.

During the French Revolution, much of the heritage of Burgundy was lost (notably through the sale of church assets) and a landed, often enterprising middle class society (metal works, coal mines) was born. Three quarters of its population still live in the countryside and new roads, canals and railways have opened up the region.

Nicéphore Niépce invented photography by trial and error near Chalon-sur-Saône between 1810 and 1820. And what an invention! The first reproduction of a glass plate photograph on paper was by Abel Niépce de Saint-Victor. The first motion pictures were taken by Beaune-born Etienne-Jules Marey.

A history of cal minig

The substratum of Burgundy is very rich. It has huge, unexploited reserves of fluorspar, uranium deposits in Grury, iron ore and oil around the Paris basin, gas in Bresse and oil shale (which is no longer extracted) in Autun. Extending from the north of Saône-et-Loire to the south of Nièvre, activity in the Blanzy coal fields peaked in the 19th century. Production grew from 30,000 tons in 1830 to 2.6 million tons per annum in the early 1960s. Over 10,000 families made their living from coal. With some 150 shafts excavated over the centuries, some of them very deep and several the scene of terrible catastrophes, mining gave rise to a particular type of interdependent society with high numbers of Polish immigrants. During this period, Montceau-les-Mines emerged as a new town.
The Yom Kippur War and a handful of opencast mines kept this activity alive until the closure of Epinac in 1966, Decize and La Machine in the Nièvre in 1974, and finally the Blanzy coal fields. However, its coal-mining past is still alive. Visit the mining museum in La Machine (Nièvre) and sites dedicated to miners near Montceau. ■

The electronic camera was invented by André Lallemand in Dijon and the first zoom was also invented in Dijon by Roger Cuvillier.

Both active and discreet, Burgundy natives invented liquid air (Louis Cailletet), discovered iodine (Bertrand Courtois), founded modern physiology (Paul Bert) and demonstrated that electrical energy could be transported (Hippolyte Fontaine).

The region's reputation for wine conceals many other activities. These various activities experienced successive and profound developments, such as the post-war arrival of foreign investors (Kodak, Philips and Hoover), their departure a few decades later, the closure of bituminous coal fields, the fortunes of the iron and steel industry, the arrival of nuclear power for military (Valduc) and civil purposes (Framatome, Areva), the survival of several small towns around one big factory (Imphy,

Above
A symbol of industrial power in Le Creusot, the power-hammer – used from 1876 to 1924 – today stands on one of the town's squares and is depicted on its coat of arms. This machine, which has a hammering weight of 100 tons and stands 69 feets tall, could open a walnut without damaging the kernel. It was used to forge huge pieces of steel.

The first photograph

Joseph Nicéphore Niépce (1765-1833) was born in Chalon-sur-Saône and spent all his life there. With an inventive mind, he and his brother developed the first internal combustion engine and dreamt up an early version of the bicycle. His first passion, however, was for heliography (or sun drawing), i.e. capturing an image on different paper media from a darkroom. The invention dates from sometime between 1816 and 1822 but the method was kept secret until 1829, when he signed an agreement with Daguerre to perfect and make use of heliography, with the latter later claiming paternity. The first known landscape photograph was fixed on 28 May 1816 after eight hours of exposure. This photograph is in the museum of Austin, Texas.

The museum of Nicéphore-Niépce, dedicated to photography and the history of photography in Chalon-sur-Saône, is worth a visit. It owes much to its former curator, Paul Jay. Afterwards, a visit to *Maison du Gras* in Saint-Loup-de-Varennes is in order. Difficult to access until relatively recently, this historic place was redesigned by Pierre-Yves Mahé to cater for visitors and is open from June to September. Here you can see Niépce's laboratory and the window from where he took the first photograph. ■

Above
Musée Niépce in Châlon-sur-Saône.

Gueugnon, Bourbon-Lancy, Montbard and Selongey) and urban development, driven by the dynamic food-processing and pharmaceutical industries.

While the number of farmers has constantly fallen, the vineyards of Burgundy continue to support many families, who pass them on from one generation to the next. Burgundy is a key breeding region, from the chicken of Bresse to the famous Charolais cattle breed. The forests are not just there to delight visitors and maintain an ecological balance either, as Burgundy is one of the leading French producers of oak, beech and Douglas fir.

Burgundy is open to the world, particularly to central and western Europe and it has close ties with Rhineland-Palatinate, Belgium and the Netherlands.

Many of its treasures were sold off in former times and are now carefully preserved in New York (Cloisters), Cleveland, Baltimore, Philadelphia and Boston (Harvard). While much of the region's heritage was saved during the 19th century, thanks notably to Viollet-le-Duc and his teams, the idea that there is a "common heritage" that should be preserved and promoted has now become widespread. Art and the art of living well make this region a high point of European civilisation.

Magny-Cours: a high-speed track

South of Nièvre, against a verdant backdrop dotted with Charolais cattle, Magny-Cours became home to the Jean-Behra racing circuit, built by Jean Bernigaud and Charles Ardoin, in 1961. The circuit soon became famous but was superseded by the Dijon-Prenois race track (1972), which hosted the French Formula One Grand Prix. Pierre Bérégovoy, former mayor of Nevers and French Prime Minister, followed in the footsteps of François Mitterrand, a personal friend of Jean Bernigaud, and allocated public funding for the large-scale renovation of Magny-Cours. The French Formula One Grand Prix took place here for several years before leaving Burgundy and indeed France. ■

Burgundy wine: an exceptional *terroir*

Left page
After the grape harvest, the vine leaves (here in Fixin and Fixey in Côte de Nuits) are awash with colour.

No other wine in the world has reigned for so long. It has a history of almost 2,000 years and is renewed from one harvest to another and from one vintage to another. It is only a few drops of good wine in the ocean of wine - but what a wine!

Above
At the foot of the rock of Solutré in Pouilly-Fuissé.

Only one in every 380 bottles of wine produced worldwide comes from Burgundy. But what a wine! Writer Raymond Dumay called it "the longest reign in history". It was probably introduced here several centuries B.C. by Gauls who had settled in Italy and it was already an ancient crop by the 4th century A.D., when it was first described. No wine has known such glory for such a long time.

The success of Burgundy wine can be traced to the perfect harmony of the *terroir* and varietals, and the work of humankind. Covering a tiny area (only 50,000 acres), Burgundy vineyards extend over three *départements*: Yonne (Chablis, Auxerrois, vineyards of Joigny, Vézelay and Tonnerre), Côte-d'Or (Côte de Nuits, Côte de Beaune, Hautes-Côtes) and Saône-et-Loire (Côte Chalonnaise, Maranges,

Above

This picture of Burgundian vines, arranged in neat rows, is fairly recent. It dates from after the phylloxera crisis and the replanting of vines on stakes (late 19th century). Before this time, vines were planted randomly in clusters.

Couchois and Mâconnais). Beaujolais, which was once part of Burgundy, is now in a separate *département* but some vineyards remain in Saône-et-Loire (Moulin-à-Vent, Saint-Amour and Fleurie). The vineyards of Nièvre (notably Pouilly-Fumé) are attached to the Loire valley. In all, 165 million bottles are produced every year, every second one exported.

Mostly raised on limestone mixed with clay and marlstone but comprising innumerable nuances, the vineyards are mainly located on slopes facing the rising sun or the south-east at altitudes of between 650

Climats of Burgundy

On 4 July 2015, UNESCO added the *Climats* of Burgundy to the World Heritage list. *Climat* is a typically Burgundian word describing all aspects of a given wine-producing area. Since the Middle Ages, around 1,250 precisely demarcated *climats* from Dijon to the region south of Beaune have formed a mosaic that is unique in the wine-making world. The most famous *climats* are Chambertin, Montrachet, Clos de Vougeot and Corton-Charlemagne. ■

and 1000 feet. They are divided into thousands of *climats*. The notion of *climat* is particular to Burgundy and defines an area of land with its own characteristic features (soil, subsoil, exposure, etc.), identified by name for centuries. Le Clos de Bèze in Gevrey-Chambertin entered into the history books as early as 640. Le Clos-Vougeot dates from the early 12th century.

Land has always prevailed over ownership. When AOC quality labels were introduced in the 1930s, other vineyards referenced ownership, brand or varietal. Burgundy, rightly, chose to reference *terroir*. The region can appear like a maze with so many *climats* but this is what guarantees the character and quality of the wine.

Excellent varietals

Wine in Burgundy is not blended but rather made from a single varietal. This is known as "*cuvée franche*". Burgundy is the birthplace of two varietals that are now known worldwide – Chardonnay (white wine) and Pinot noir (red wine) – and they are the focus of wine making here today. In the Mâconnais, they produce Gamay Noir à Jus Blanc, similar to Beaujolais wine, and a dry white wine, Aligoté.

Other red wines include Romanée Conti, Chambertin, Clos-Vougeot and Corton. Covering 8,000 ha, Pinot noir is the most delicate of the red wine varietals (its juice is colourless and the skin of the grape provides its colour during the wine-making process). It produces sumptuous wines, that are rich and profound, complex

Below
Grape harvest in Côte de Beaune.

Measurements

Two hundred years after the French Revolution, Burgundy winemakers continue to use their own system of measurement. An *ouvrée* equals 4.285 acres. There are about 24 *ouvrées* in one hectare. When selling wine properties, the *ouvrée*, rather than the hectare, is the unit of measurement. Eight *ouvrées* make one *journal*, which covers 34.284 acres. Now standardised, these units once varied from village to village. In the Mâconnais, they also have the *coupée* (3.96 acres). Here there is no talk of casks, the oak barrels are known as *pièces*: 228 litres in Côte-d'Or and Côte Chalonnaise, i.e. exactly 300 bottles, and 215 litres in the Mâconnais. *Feuillettes* contain 114 litres everywhere except in Chablis (136 litres) and the Mâconnais (108 litres). *Quartants* contain 57 litres (54 in the Mâconnais). Vats are known as *cuveries* in Côte-d'Or, *cuvages* in the Mâconnais and Beaujolais, and *tinaillers*, also in Beaujolais. ■

Opposite

Château de Corton-André in Aloxe-Corton.

and subtle. Beurot and Liébault are variants of *Noirien* or Pinot noir, and, as is the case for all varietals, there are many clones that are constantly being improved.

Other white wines include Montrachet, Chablis, Meursault and Pouilly-Fuissé. With 22,240 acres in Burgundy, Chardonnay (known as Beaunois in Chablis) provides unity without sinking into uniformity as there are a thousand variations on the same theme. Smooth and dry, firm and silky, it expresses all the graces backed up by strong character. Vigorous and generous, this varietal is frost-resistant.

Gamay Noir à Jus Blanc gives a tasty, light, fruity red wine. Robust and fruitful, it prefers the acid soil of south Burgundy (6,000 acres, all vineyards combined) and the Beaujolais. It has long rivalled Pinot noir. It is easier to produce more Gamay wine, making it more profitable for winemakers, whereas the abbeys and large demesnes have traditionally favoured Pinot noir, which is better but which has a lower yield and therefore revenue is less assured. Pinot and Gamay engaged in a class war from the Middle Ages but this has now abated.

Aligoté is to Chardonnay what Gamay is to Pinot. It is a simpler white wine, lively, sharp as flint and fresh as the spring breeze. Production of this good-natured varietal extends over 3,000 acres and, in Bouzeron (Côte chalonnaise) it even has its own *appellation*. Hautes-Côtes is the perfect site for this varietal.

A handful of ancient varietals remain in Yonne: Melon de Bourgogne (Muscadet Nantais) in Vézelay, Sauvignon de Saint-Bris and Le Sacy for white wines, and for red wines, César, which is still grown in Irancy.

Opposite

Meursault cellars.

The personality of each vintage

Each vintage has its own characteristics. This can be more or less successful and more or less full-bodied. Various factors, particularly climate conditions, explain these differences, which change over time for different vintages. With a few notable exceptions, Burgundy wines are not meant to be consumed within months of harvesting. They must be laid down. They are bottled after one or two years. Most often, Burgundy wine only comes into its own after three to four years. It is a wine for laying down, often superb after ten to fifteen years and absolutely wonderful after 50 years (now is the right time to drink the 1947 and 1949 vintages).

Finally, wine is the work of humankind. The influence of the winemaker – the wine growers themselves, with the assistance of an oenologist – is a determining factor. Some winemakers sell their wines directly, in which case it is called *vin de propriété*, some sell them onsite to wine producers and merchants for laying down and marketing, and others send their wines to a cooperative (Chablis, Hautes-Côtes and Saône-et-Loire).

La descente de cave wine tasting

A traditional Burgundian ritual, *la descente de cave* involves a tasting accompanied by personal commentary. This takes place in the cellar of the property, where the wine is laid down by producers or wine merchants. This is no frivolous activity – tasting is a serious business. The wine is tasted in a glass, or even better in a special wine-tasting cup known as *tâtevin*. Often, visitors sample young wines directly from the barrel and a few bottles of more mature wines are opened. This is an opportunity to compare vintages while learning about the art of wine tasting.

Burgundy has developed a precise and evocative vocabulary to refer to the infinite nuances of colour (clarity, colour, reflections, etc.), of aromas (vegetal, floral, fruit, mineral, etc.) and finish (body, concentration, length of finish, etc.). The ideal to attain is complexity.

The wine auction of the *hospices de Beaune*

Founded by Nicolas Rolin in 1443, the *Hôtel-Dieu* (hospital) of Beaune owns a large wine estate (almost 150 acres), built up over the years from donations. It includes Côte de Beaune, Côte de Nuits and the vineyard of Pouilly-Fuissé. Since 1859, the hospice wines have been sold at auction on the third Sunday of November after the wine harvest. "The largest charity sale in the world" has become a major event, setting prices much higher than the market. This event is one of three comprising the *Trois Glorieuses* weekend. The day before, there is a chapter of the *Confrérie des Chevaliers du Tastevin*. The day after is the *Paulée de Meursault*, a lunch to celebrate the end of the wine harvest and a literary prize. The *Hospices de Nuits-Saint-Georges* also auction off their wines, in the Spring following the harvest. ■

Above

Les Cordeliers cellar, Beaune.

The pyramid of *appellations*

Based on the concept of origin, here more than elsewhere, Burgundy has one quarter of all French AOC quality labels, about 110 out of a total of 400. This is hardly surprising as in Burgundy each wine carries its own name.

Representing 1% of total production, there are 32 *grands crus* in Côte-d'Or and another in Chablis, which has seven *climats*. This is the "crème de la crème" of Burgundy *appellations*. Examples include Chablis, Grand cru Grenouille, Clos de Bèze, Chambertin, Corton-Charlemagne and Bâtard-Montrachet.

Premiers crus represent 11% of total production. These are known as *AOC communales* when classified as *premiers crus* (this is the case for 561 *climats*). Examples include Chablis-Mont de Milieu, Nuits-Saint-Georges-Les Saint-Georges, Beaune-Grèves and Mercurey-Clos du Roi.

The other *AOC communales* (fifty-three in total) represent 23% of production and make up *appellations* known as *Villages*. The name of the

Above
Château de Gevrey-Chambertin, the former wine cellar of the Cluny monks.

Below
Château Marey-Monge, Pommard.

climat often features on the label. Examples include Chablis, Gevrey-Chambertin, Pommard, Rully and Pouilly-Fuissé. Petit-Chablis is an *AOC communale*.

Finally, 65% of production is accounted for by *AOC régionales*. There are currently twenty-two of these, including Bourgogne and Mâcon.

There are, therefore three levels of *appellation*: *grands crus*, *appellations communales* (*Villages* and *premiers crus*) sometimes followed by the *climat*, and *appellations régionales* (sometimes incorrectly referred to as "generic"). These refer to the varietal (Bourgogne Aligoté, Bourgogne Passe-tout-grain, made from at least one third Pinot grapes, and Gamay), to the way the wine is made (Crémant de Bourgogne), or to its geographical origin (Bourgogne Chitry, Bourgogne Hautes-

Above
The Château de Savigny-lès-Beaune boasts an impressive collection of old planes in its grounds.

The *Confrérie des Chevaliers du Tastevin*

There are now innumerable wine and food brotherhoods. Founded in 1934, the *Confrérie des Chevaliers du Tastevin* is the oldest of them all. The idea in fact comes from Burgundy.

At the time, wine was not selling well. A few inhabitants from Nuits-Saint-Georges decided to react, saying: "If nobody wants our wine, let's invite a few friends round and drink it together!" And so the brotherhood was set up and it became an overnight success. Members are inducted by being struck three times on the shoulder with a vine stock ("by Noah, father of the vine, by Bacchus, god of wine, by Saint Vincent, patron saint of wine growers") and go on to become the best publicists of Burgundy wine. This is none other than the beginning of public relations!

The *Confrérie des Chevaliers du Tastevin* holds around twenty meetings, or chapters, every year at the Château du Clos-Vougeot, which it acquired in 1944. The brotherhood has some 10,000 members and many outposts all over the world. It has often been innovative, developing the *Tastevinage*, a strictly blind tasting of wines known as *Tastevinés* that "you would offer your friends" and serve at the *Saint-Vincent Tournante*, or revolving Saint Vincent, festival.

Most wine-producing villages have had a mutual aid society since the 19th century. Although often secular, these are generally under the patronage of Saint Vincent. Any wine grower who is unable to work because of an accident or illness receives aid from his or her fellow members. The statue of their patron saint is hosted by different families in turn and thus the saint "tourne", or "passes from village to village". In 1937, the *Confrérie des Chevaliers du Tastevin* thought up the annual gathering in Burgundy of all the brotherhoods under the patronage of Saint Vincent, which is held on the last Saturday of January, each time in a different village. The appointed village has several years to prepare for the event – known as the *Saint-Vincent tournante* – and it is the most magnificent of all wine-growers' festivals.

There have been many other brotherhoods in Burgundy, for example Piliers chablisiens, Trois Ceps, Foudres du Tonnerrois, Veilleurs de Nuits, Cousinerie de Bourgogne in Savigny-lès-Beaune, Bailliage de Pommard, Grumeurs de Santenay, Disciples de la Chanteflûte in Mercurey and Compagnons de Saint-Vincent in the Mâconnais. ■

Crémant de Bourgogne

Although Burgundy has been producing sparkling wines since the early nineteenth century (Alfred de Musset mentions Bourgogne Mousseux in a poem dated 1830), the appellation Crémant de Bourgogne first recognised in 1975 for white and rosé has stamped these wines with the mark of excellence. In the mid-2010s, production stands at 20 million bottles. ■

Above and below
One of the four presses of the Château du Clos de Vougeot, a prestigious Burgundian *table d'hôtes*. The French historian Gaston Roupnel remarked, "here everyone toasts to the health of France".

Côtes de Nuits and Hautes-Côtes de Beaune, and Bourgogne Côte Chalonnaise). Whether red, white or rosé, the *appellation* is Bourgogne with no other indication on the label, except sometimes the *climat* (Montre-Cul, for example, in Dijon-Chenôve).

Château du Clos de Vougeot

Both a vineyard and a wine, this wine-making castle is the epitome of Burgundy. It was founded by the Abbey of Cîteaux and is the most prestigious *table d'hôte* in France, thanks to the *Confrérie des Chevaliers du Tastevin*, which holds its chapters here. Though immense, this square castle is not out of place here. In the spirit of the Burgundy Renaissance, the castle cloister (which much impressed Rabelais) is used as a fermentation room and its cellar, as a storage room. Surrounded by enor-

mous roofs that almost reach the ground, the interior courtyard is mysterious and inviting.

Hameau du Vin (Romanèche-Thorins, Saône-et-Loire)

In the south of Saône-et-Loire, on the border with Beaujolais, Hameau du Vin was founded in 1993 by Georges Dubœuf, one of the fathers of Beaujolais Nouveau. Housed in a former railway station, there are many attractions for visitors in this leisure park, dedicated to wine and vine in the Mâconnais and Beaujolais (models, slide shows, a puppet theatre, 3D film, old posters, wax works, etc.). Romanèche-Thorins also has a zoo and leisure park (Touroparc) opened in 1961 by René Livet.

The Imaginarium

The Imaginarium in Nuits-Saint-Georges (Côte-d'Or) was set up in 2006 by Maison Louis Bouillot/Jean-Claude Boisset and features an interactive tour of the world of sparkling wines (Crémant de Bourgogne). The huge underground quarries of Bailly (Yonne) in Auxerrois is another site dedicated to this sparkling wine.

Above and below left
The Hameau du Vin in Romanèche-Thorins. Burgundy wine is matured in oak barrels for one or two years before being bottled.

Below
Le Cassissium in Nuits-Saint-Georges.

Anis
de l'Abbaye
de
Flavigny
Véritable Marque des Anis
VENTE ICI

A food lover's paradise

Burgundy is where the art and pleasure of living meet, and where taste, *terroirs*, colours, aromas and flavours abound.

Left page
Flavigny aniseed.

Opposite
Dijon mustard.
Photo Didier Benaouda.

Over two hundred years ago, gastronomic writer Brillat-Savarin recognised that Burgundians have "bowels of silk", so enamoured were they of fine cuisine. The art of fine eating has been perfected here. When you go to the *Hôtel de ville* in Dijon, you are fed in the ducal kitchens, a model of architectural design where fabulous banquets were once prepared for the great Dukes of Burgundy. Recipes are handed down through the generations as if they were the most precious family secrets.

Colours, aromas and flavours

Just like France as a whole, Burgundy has its own culinary preferences. Its cuisine is above all else a culture, made of colours, aromas and flavours – a thousand and one culinary delights. Conversation is part of the art of fine eating. Eating is a contemplative activity and talk is

Photo Didier Benaouda

complementary. Visitors should avoid arriving somewhere at 11.45 am without notice, as the cook needs time to prepare food for his or her guests, time to go to the market and to pick a bottle from the cellar to honour them with. In short, living well requires time!

Burgundy has a wonderful heritage. The people of Burgundy are faithful to this heritage, to the soil, the climate, the countryside, traditions, local customs and *appellations d'origine*. Wine is not the only produce here, there are cereals, vegetables, fine Charolais beef and Bresse chicken, red fruit (cherry, redcurrant, raspberry and strawberry), black fruit (blackcurrant and blackberry) and many cheeses. Often this high-quality produce bears its origin, such as the Appoigny gherkin, the Auxonne onion, the Auxerrois cherry or the blackcurrant from Hautes-Côtes.

Thanks to expert farming, this produce is excellent. It represents the very soul of Burgundy, because it took centuries, for example, to develop the great Charolais breed, which originates in the Charolais Brionnais and Nivernais. This genetic treasure is exported worldwide and provides succulent, marbled meat straight from the meadows. Those white spots you see everywhere in the countryside are some of the 1,400,000 heads of cattle in this region. Similarly, Bresse chicken, with its blue feet, white feathers and red crest, although not necessarily raised using strictly traditional methods, is always free-range. If you haven't tasted Bresse capon, you haven't lived!

The Burgundy menu

A traditional meal starts in Burgundy with an aperitif, accompanied by *gougères*, warm cheese pastries and small ramekins of cheese. For starters, you may be served a dozen snails cooked in a thousand different ways, ham sprinkled with chopped parsley or *œufs en meurette* (eggs in red wine sauce). The fish dish is next with Burgundian fish stew, called *pauchouse*, combining carp, tench and pike in white wine. For the meat dish, expect a Burgundy hotpot, beef bourguignon, saddle of hare "à la Piron" (with raisins and cream), ham "à la Nuitonne" (cooked in Nuits St-Georges), ham with cream, saupiquet (a spicy stew with Saulieu and Montberdois) or coq au vin. *Andouillette* (chitterling sausage made with Chablis, Clamecy or Mâconnais wine) is also highly prized here.

Burgundy also boasts a fine cheese platter. The abbeys of Cîteaux and Pierre-qui-Vire continue to uphold this wonderful monastic tradition, and Epoisses and its variants (ami du Chambertin), Soumaintrain and Aisy cendré are all reputed. There are also some excellent goat's cheeses, particularly in the Mâconnais (Chèvreton, Bouton de culotte).

For dessert, you will perhaps be offered a Vacherin with blackcurrant or a *Poire Belle Dijonnaise* (pear in red wine). Afterwards, marc brandy, fine de Bourgogne or sloe gin are served. Apart from the excellent agricultural produce available, Burgundians favour blackcurrant, mustard and *pain d'épice* in their cooking. Burgundy cuisine is naturally highly inventive and the traditional recipe book is constantly being updated ■

Blackcurrant, mustard and *pain d'épice*

Of the many Burgundy specialities, several have attained an international reputation, such as the famous aniseed of Flavigny and nougatine from Nevers.

There are many associations that celebrate the snail (beloved of writer Henri Vincenot), the onion and the *cacou* (a clafoutis made with unstoned cherries, a speciality of Paray-le-Monial). Every year during the Dijon international gastronomy fair, all the bigwigs of French gastronomy come here to share their knowledge. In 1997, the French National Centre for

Don't miss

Arnay-le-Duc (Côte-d'Or): *Maison des Arts de la table* in the former *Hospice Saint-Pierre*, which presents a remarkable exhibition every year on a gourmet theme.

Auxerre (Yonne): *Museum Leblanc-Duvernoy* and its china collection.

Beaune (Côte-d'Or): Mustard museum created by mustard manufacturer Fallot;

Charolles (Saône-et-Loire): Traditional china (*bleu de Charolles*) and exhibitions on Charolais cattle.

Dijon: *Musée de la Vie bourguignonne*; Mustard museum created by Amora-Maille; the 19th-century covered market and open-air market (held on Tuesday, Friday and Saturday mornings) and the Dijon international gastronomy fair.

Glux-en-Glenne (Nièvre): Redcurrant festival in August.

Longchamp (Côte-d'Or): A reference in the art of eating well.

Louhans (Saône-et-Loire): Poultry market on Mondays and fairs.

Mâcon (Saône-et-Loire): French national wine fair in May.

Magny-Cours (Nièvre): Exhibitions on Charolais cattle.

Marcigny (Saône-et-Loire): Turkey and goose market on the second Monday in December.

Moulins-Engilbert (Nièvre): Livestock market on Mondays and Tuesdays.

Nevers (Nièvre): Frédéric-Blandin museum and its Nevers china collections (bleu de Nevers).

Nuits-Saint-Georges (Côte-d'Or): The Cassissium, created by Maison Védrenne (a renowned liqueur maker), is a very attractive site dedicated to black-currant, which is abundant throughout Hautes-Côtes and Côte de Nuits. This is a lively museum where visitors can taste this little black fruit.

Pierre-de-Bresse (Saône-et-Loire): Ecomuseum.

Pouilly-sur-Loire (Nièvre): Wine fair in August.

Reulle-Vergy (Côte-d'Or): Museum of Arts and Traditions of Hautes-Côtes.

Romenay (Saône-et-Loire): *Musée du Terroir et de la Volaille* (poultry museum).

Saint-Christophe-en-Brionnais (Saône-et-Loire): Livestock market (early Thursday morning).

Saulieu (Côte-d'Or): The *Journées gourmandes* every year in Spring, museum, *Journées du charolais* in August.

Tournus (Saône-et-Loire): *Musée Perrin-de-Puycousin* (popular arts and traditions of Tournugeois, Mâconnais and Bresse).

Verdun-sur-le-Doubs (Saône-et-Loire): *Maison du Blé et du Pain* (bread museum). ■

Scientific Research set up the European Centre for Taste Sciences to develop research that was already underway (particularly in aromas).

Where does kir come from?

Most restaurants nowadays offer kir or kir royal as an aperitif. Canon Félix Kir (1876-1968), mayor of Dijon, who was first elected at the age of 69 and remained in office for twenty-three years, used to offer this drink to his guests. It comprised one third *crème de cassis* from Dijon and two thirds Aligoté, a dry white wine as sharp as the spring breeze. These two products from Hautes-Côtes go very well together. Canon Kir gave his name, which is easy to remember, to this aperitif. Of course, it probably existed well before his time but had no name. Aligoté was later replaced by Crémant de Bourgogne, a sparkling wine. ■

Contents

Editor: Jérôme Le Bihan
Editorial Coordination: Isabelle Rousseau
Layout: Éditions Ouest-France graphic studio
Cartography: Patrick Mérienne
Photoengraving: Nord Compo, Villeneuve d'Ascq (59)
Printing: Pollina, Luçon (85)

ISBN 978-2-7373-7082-3
Legal deposit: March 2016
Publisher no: 8176.01.0,5.03.16

Printed in France
www.editionsouestfrance.fr